CELLO POSITION HANDBOOK, VOLUME 1

HALLEY FEASTER

Online Video

Download
dv.melbay.com/30990

YouTube
www.melbay.com/30990V

WWW.MELBAY.COM

Contents

Welcome
to the
Cello Position Handbook
Volume 1

Most novice cello students start in first position marked with finger tapes. As we advance, we are expected to learn to shift out of first position, but the focus is often on the movement of the shift rather than on intonation or the notes available in the new position. In this book, we'll examine each left-hand position on the cello, independent from shifting.

With my students, I have seen that learning shifting and fully understanding positions one at a time leads to more thorough comprehension of the cello fingerboard as well as a more well-rounded player.

The Cello Position Handbook introduces all twelve fingerboard positions, showing the student which notes are available in each one and providing short exercises and/or excerpts for practice without unnecessary shifting. Students can also play along with the companion video, in which I briefly describe each position and play through every exercise and excerpt.

On completing this book, students will be familiar with the notes available in each position, comfortable in shifting to them, and ready to apply this knowledge as they expand their repertoires.

First Position

Before starting Lesson 1, make sure you are familiar with First Position and First Extended Position as depicted here.

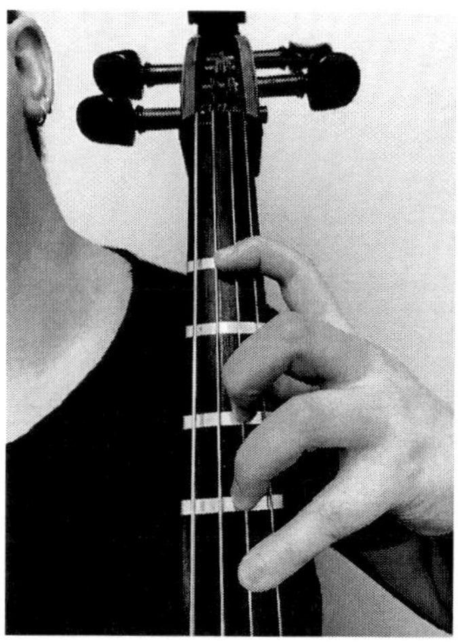

First Extended Position

Lesson 1
Half Position

	Finger 1	Finger 2	Finger 3	Finger 4
A String	B♭	B	C	D♭
D String	E♭	E	F	G♭
G String	A♭	A	B♭	B
C String	D♭	D	E♭	E

In Half Position, on the D string, your first finger goes on E♭ (or D♯), second finger on E, third finger on F, and fourth finger on F♯ (or G♭).

We won't reach the fourth finger tape in this position.

Each finger will be a half step apart.

Lesson 1
Exercises in Half Position

A

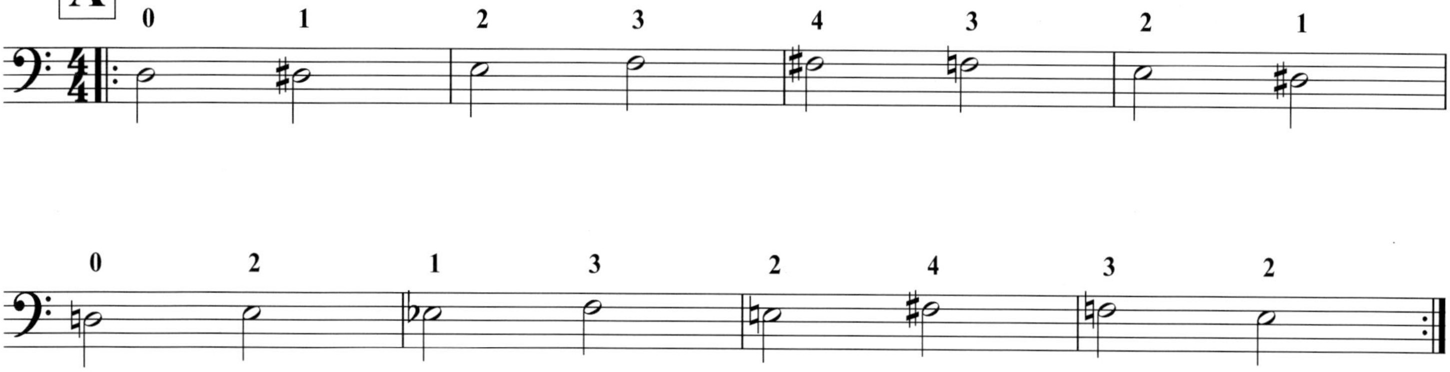

B

C

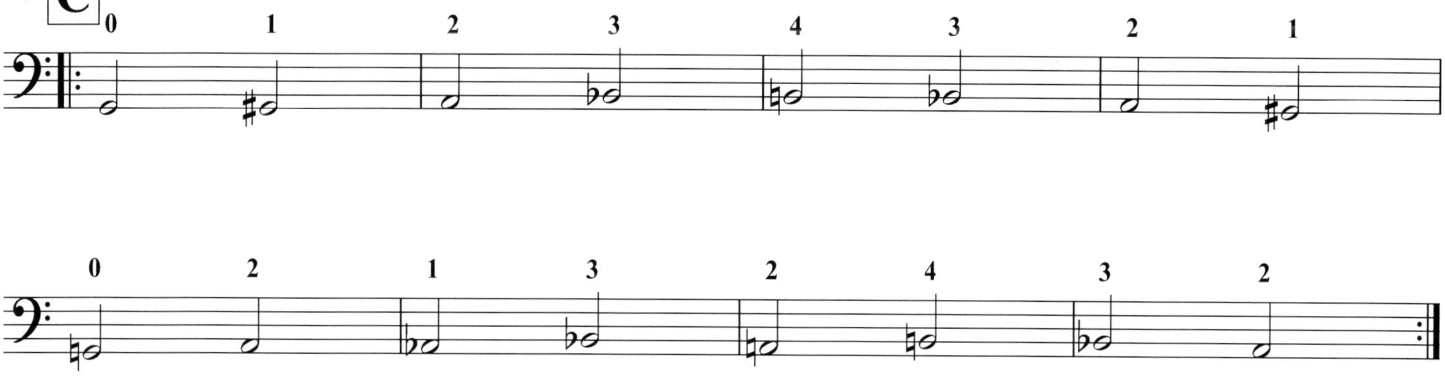

D

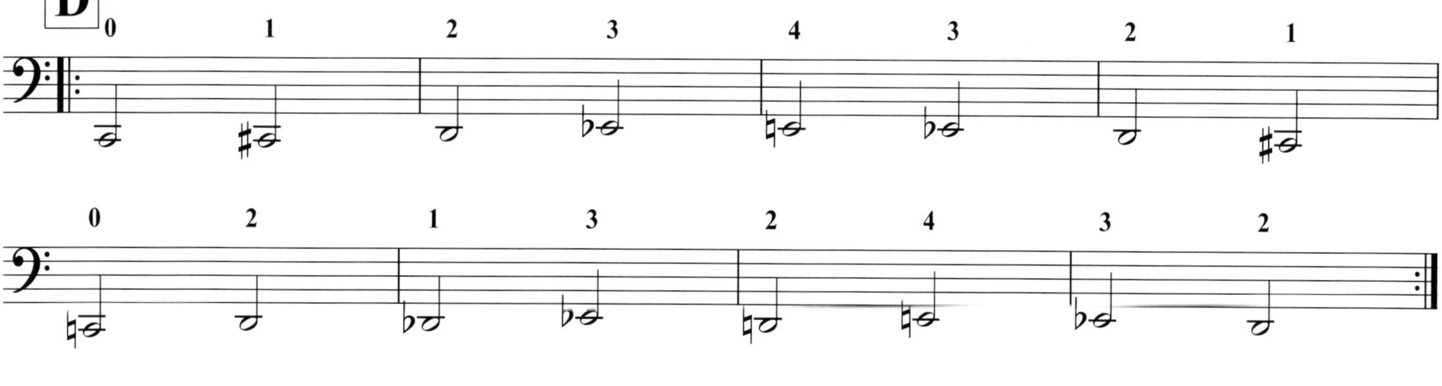

E
F
G
H
I

J

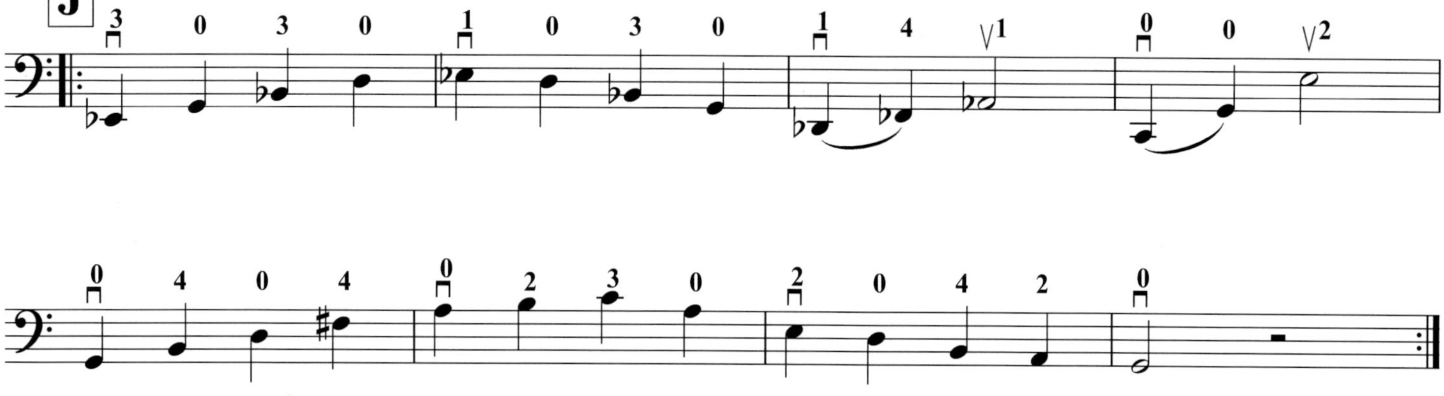

K

L

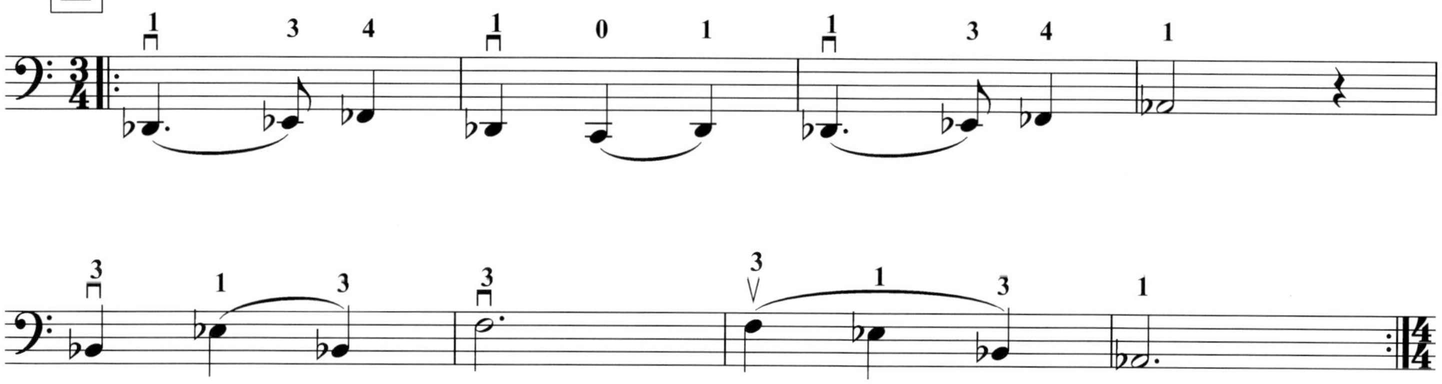

M from *The Fiddling Cellist* - "Fire on the Mountain"

N from *The Fiddling Cellist* - "Cherokee Shuffle" duet

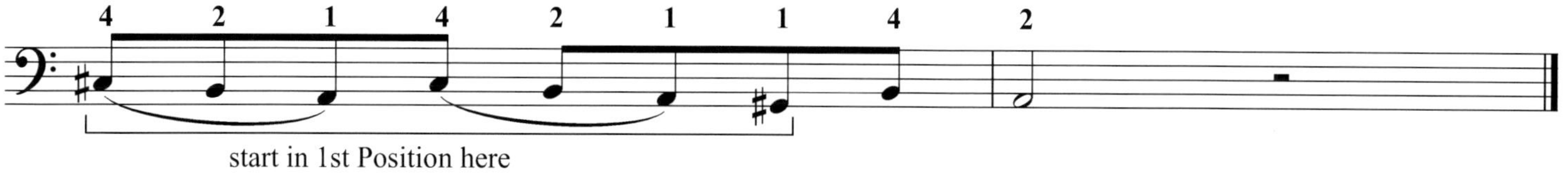

O from *Brahms Cello Sonata - Opus 38, No. 1, Mvt. 1*

Lesson 2
Half Extended Position

	Finger 1	Finger 2	Finger 3	Finger 4
A String	B♭	C	C♯	D
D String	E♭	F	F♯	G
G String	A♭	B♭	B	C
C String	D♭	E♭	E	F

In Half Extended Position, on the D string, your first finger goes on E♭ (or D♯), second finger on F, third finger on F♯, and fourth finger on G.

Keep in mind: This is very much like First Position, with your 2nd, 3rd, and 4th fingers on their respective tapes. The difference is that your 1st finger will be pointed back towards the nut, leaving your 1st finger tape empty.

Lesson 2
Exercises in Half Extended Position

A

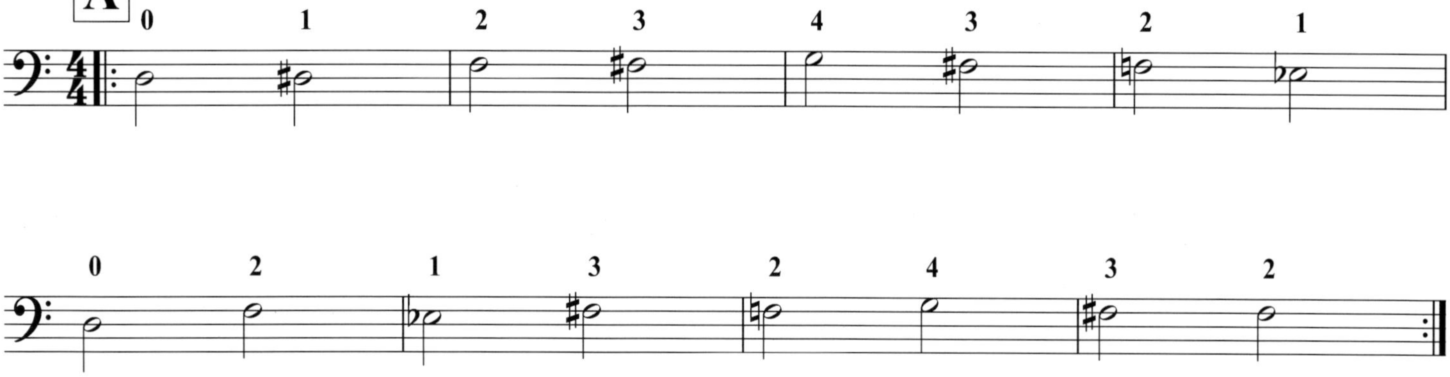

B

C

D

E
F
G
H
I

J

K from *101 Easy Songs for Cello* - "Bringing In the Sheaves"

L from *101 Easy Songs for Cello* - "Come Back to Sorrento"

M from *101 Easy Songs for Cello* - "Down at the Station"

N from *101 Easy Songs for Cello* - "Go Tell It on the Mountain"

O from *101 Easy Songs for Cello* - "In the Good Old Summertime"

P from *Breval Cello Sonata - Opus 40, No. 2, Mvt. 2*

Lesson 3
Low Second Position

	Finger 1	Finger 2	Finger 3	Finger 4
A String	C	C♯	D	E♭
D String	F	F♯	G	A♭
G String	B♭	B	C	D♭
C String	E♭	E	F	G♭

In Low Second Position on the D string, your first finger goes on F, second finger on F♯ (G♭), third finger on G, and fourth finger on G♯ (A♭).

Keep in mind: your 3rd finger is on the 4th finger tape!

Lesson 3
Exercises in Low Second Position

A

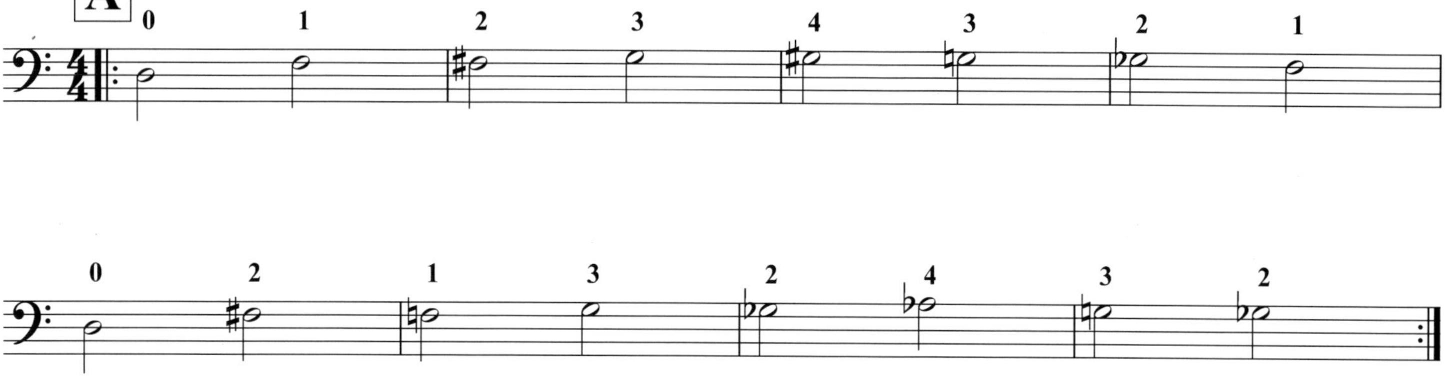

B

C

D

E
F
G
H
I

J

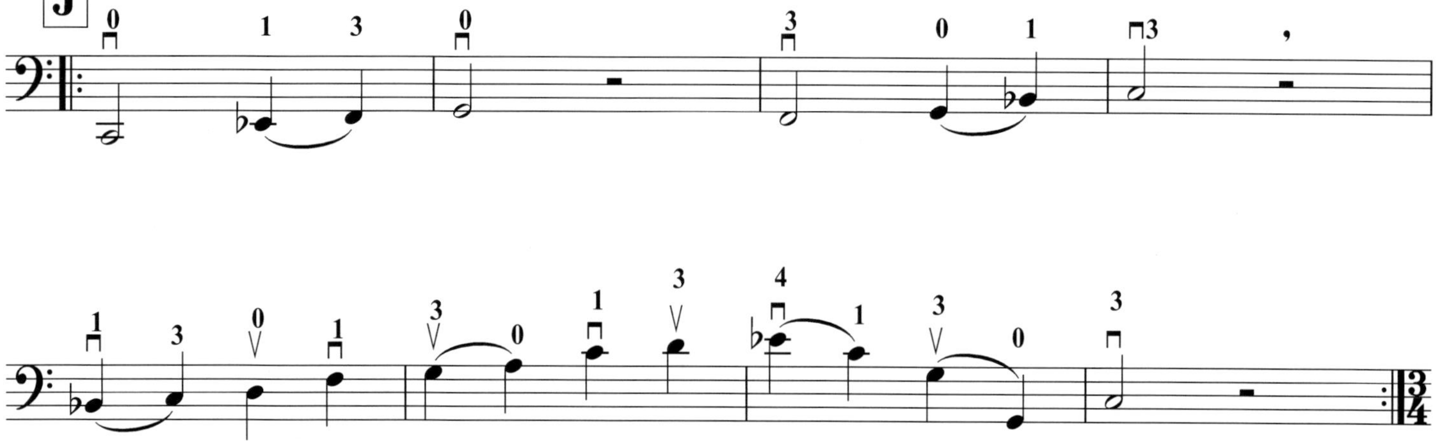

K

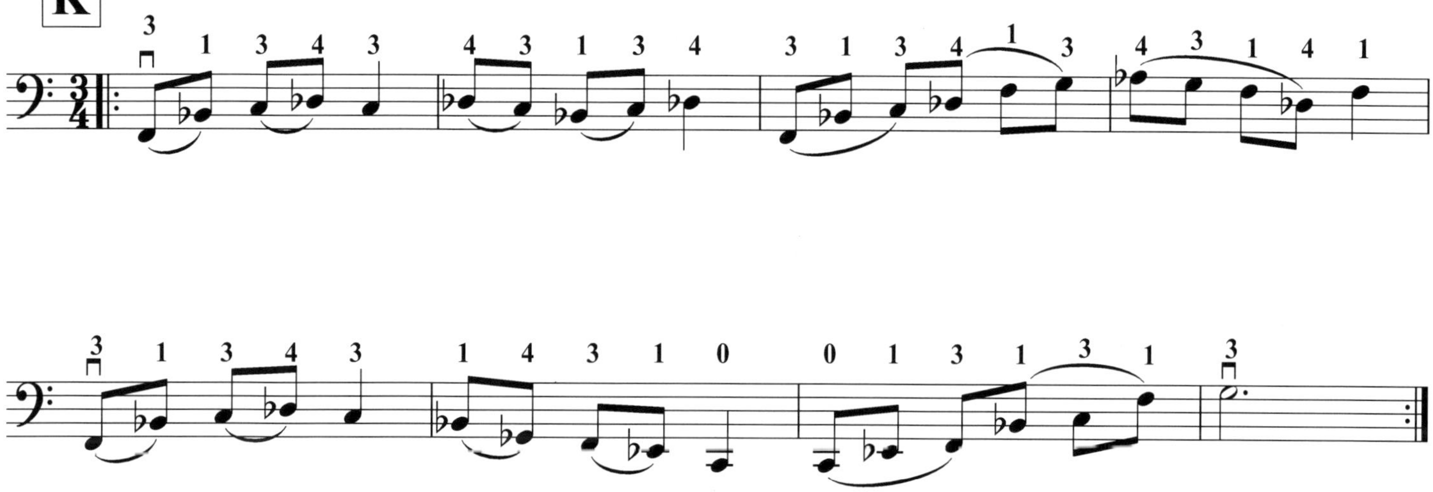

L from *Eccles Cello Sonata in G Minor - Mvt. 2*

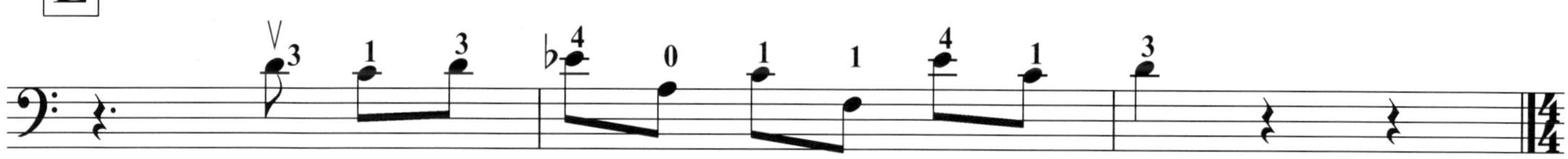

M from *Brahms Cello Sonata - Opus 38, No. 1, Mvt. 1*

N from *Fauré Élégie, Op. 24*

Lesson 4
Low Second Extended Position

	Finger 1	Finger 2	Finger 3	Finger 4
A String	C	D	E♭	E
D String	F	G	A♭	A
G String	B♭	C	D♭	D
C String	E♭	F	G♭	G

In Low Second Extended Position on the D string, your first finger goes on F, second finger stretches a whole step to G, third finger on G♯ (A♭), and fourth finger on A.

Each finger will be a half step apart, with the exception of the first and second finger, which will stretch a whole step.

Keep in mind: In this position, your 4th finger will be able to replace open strings! 4th finger on A on the D string = open A.

Lesson 4
Exercises in Low Second Extended Position

A

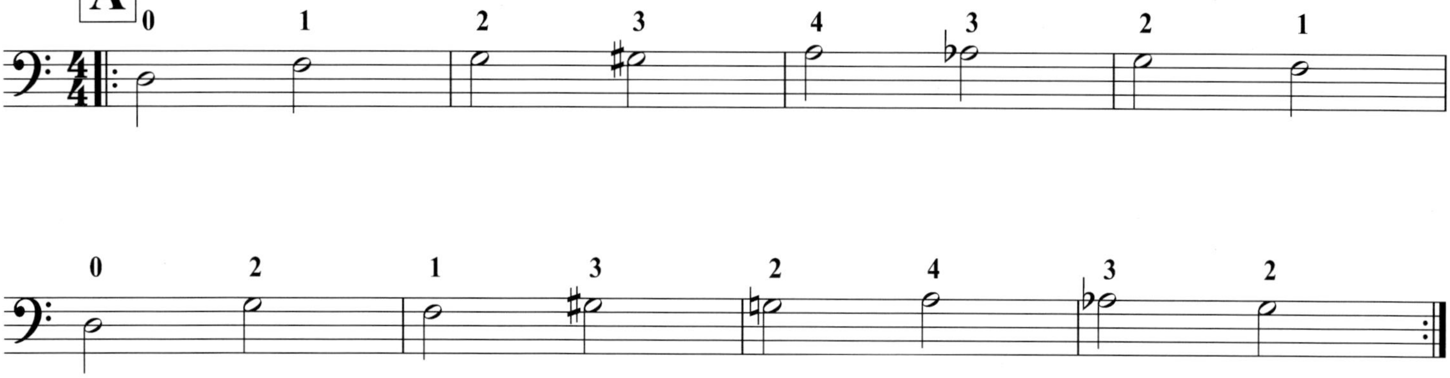

B

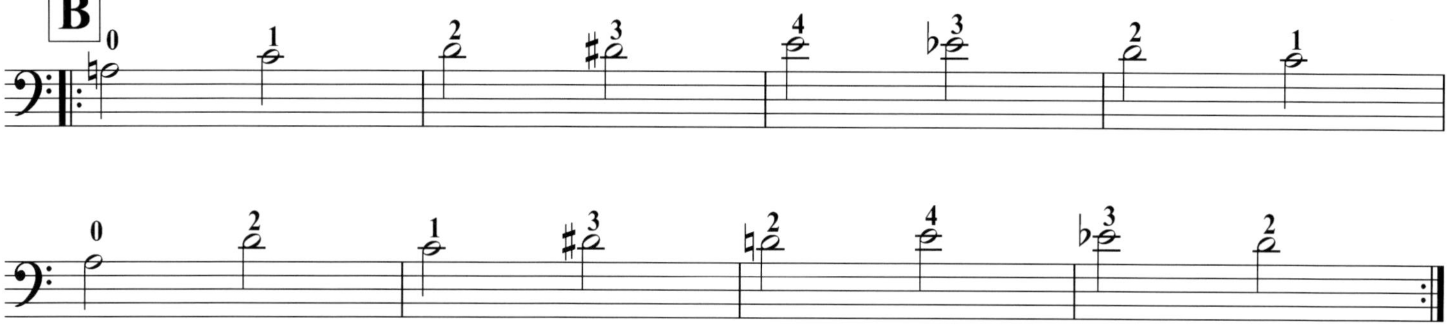

C

D

E
F
G
H
I

J

K

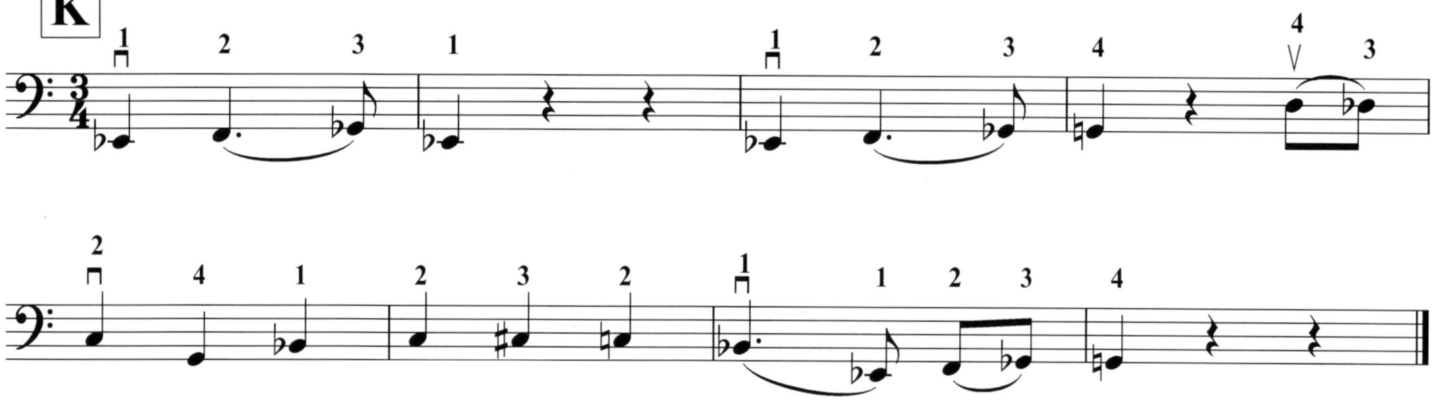

L from *The Fiddling Cellist* - "Star of the County Down" duet

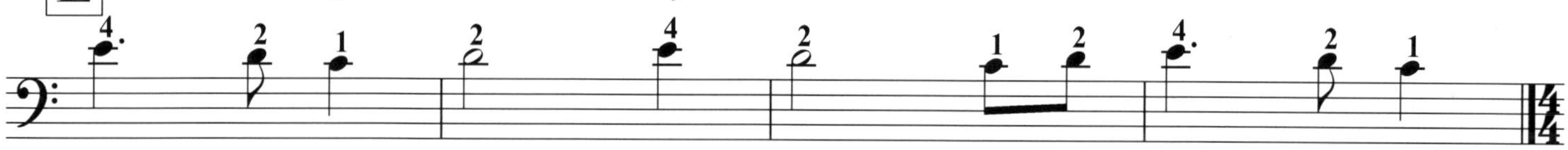

M from *The Fiddling Cellist* - "Elzic's Farewell"

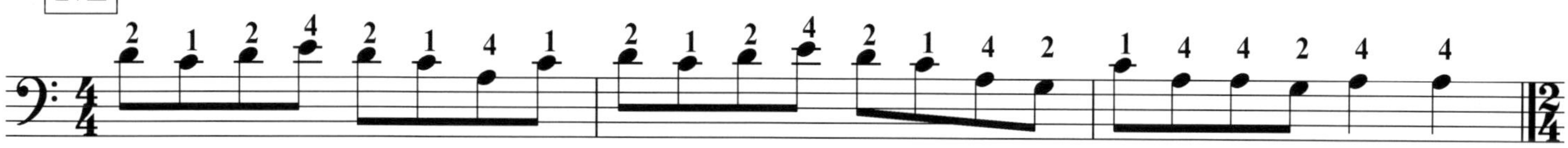

N from *Breval Cello Sonata - Opus 40, No. 2, Mvt. 2*

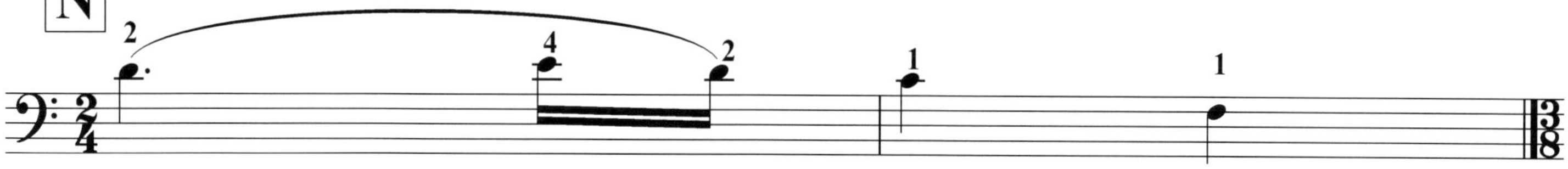

O from *J. S. Bach Cello Suite No. 3, Gigue*

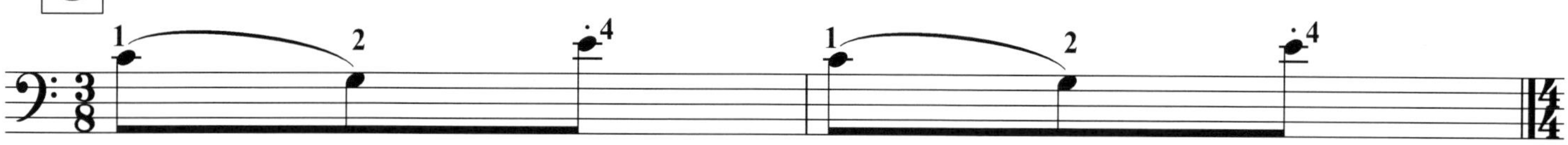

P from *Brahms Cello Sonata - Opus 38 No. 1, Mvt. 1*

Lesson 5
High Second Position

	Finger 1	Finger 2	Finger 3	Finger 4
A String	C♯	D	E♭	E
D String	F♯	G	A♭	A
G String	B	C	D♭	D
C String	E	F	G♭	G

In High Second Position on the D string, your first finger goes on F♯ (G♭), second finger on G, third finger on G♯ (A♭), and fourth finger on A.

Each finger will be a half step apart.

Keep in mind: Your 4th finger is still on the same note as in Low Second Extended Position, and your 1st finger is on your 3rd finger tape.

Lesson 5
Exercises in High Second Position

A

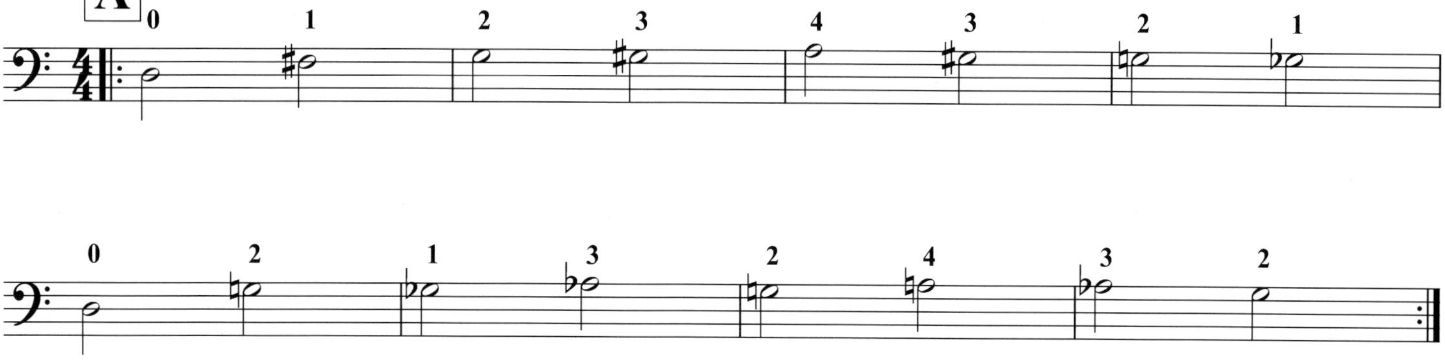

B

C

D

E

F

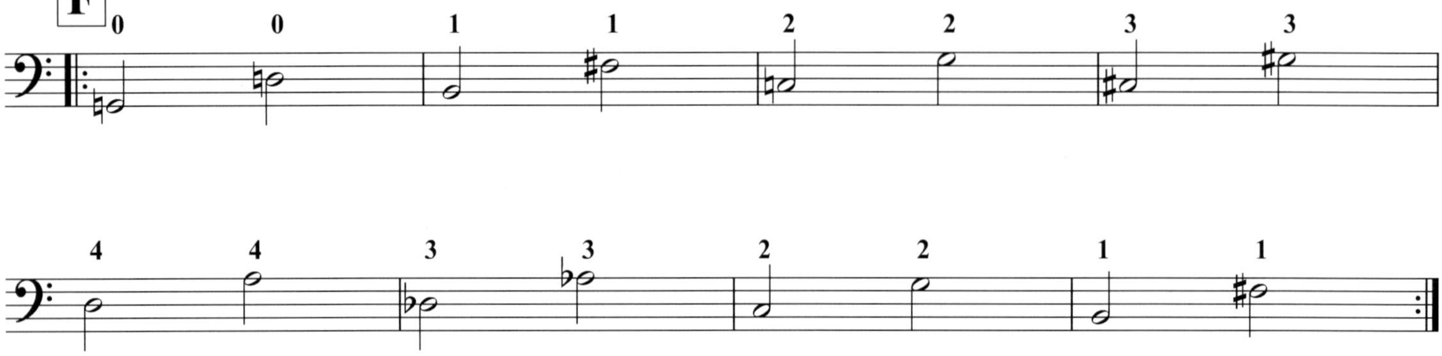

G

H

I

J

K from *Cello Solo Pieces* - "Prelude"

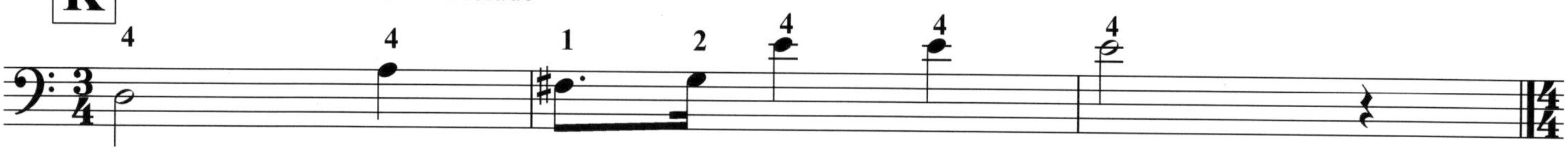

L from *The Fiddling Cellist* - "Fisher's Hornpipe" duet

M from *101 Easy Songs for Cello* - "Ode to Joy"

N from *101 Easy Songs for Cello* - "O Day Full of Grace"

O from *101 Easy Songs for Cello* - "Southern Roses"

P from *Easy Classics for Cello* - "Sleeping Beauty Waltz"

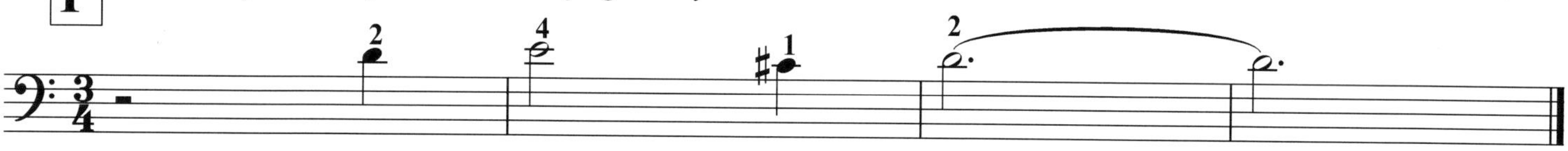

Q from *J.S. Bach Cello Suite No. 1, Mvt. 1*

Lesson 6
High Second Extended Position

	Finger 1	Finger 2	Finger 3	Finger 4
A String	C♯	D♯	E	F
D String	F♯	G♯	A	B♭
G String	B	C♯	D	E♭
C String	E	F♯	G	A♭

In High Second Extended Position on the D string, your first finger goes on F♯, second finger stretches a whole step to G♯ (A♭), third finger on A, and fourth finger on B♭ (A♯).

Each finger will be a half step apart, with the exception of the first and second finger, which will stretch a whole step.

Keep in mind: In this position, your 3rd finger is now the one replacing open strings! Your 1st finger is still on the 3rd finger tape.

Lesson 6
Exercises in High Second Extended Position

A

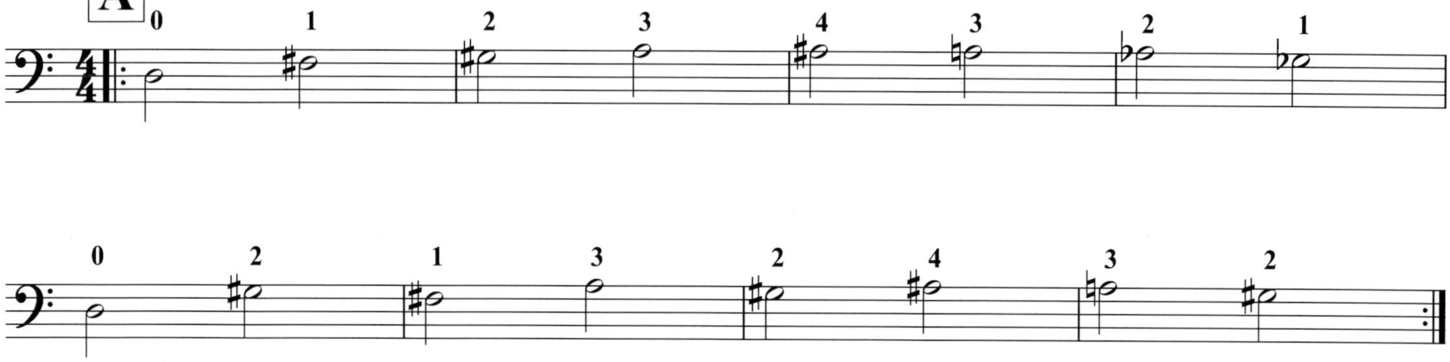

B

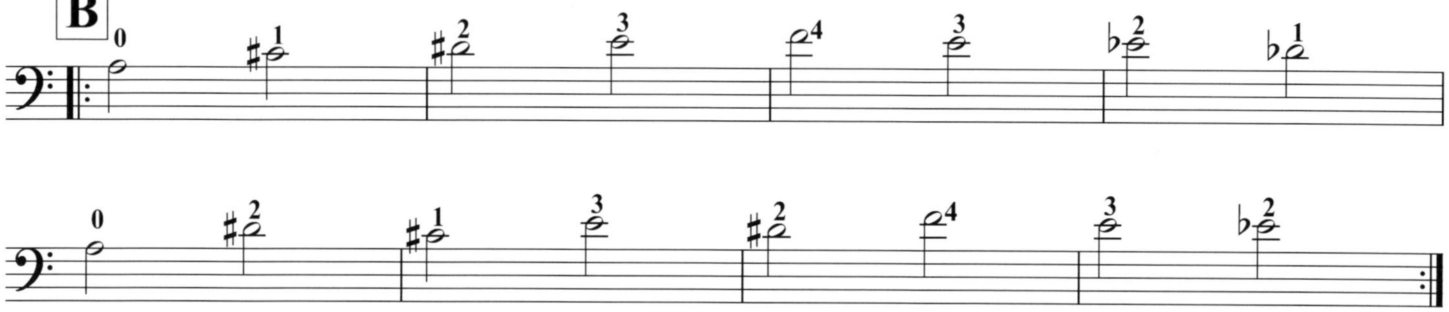

C

D

E

F

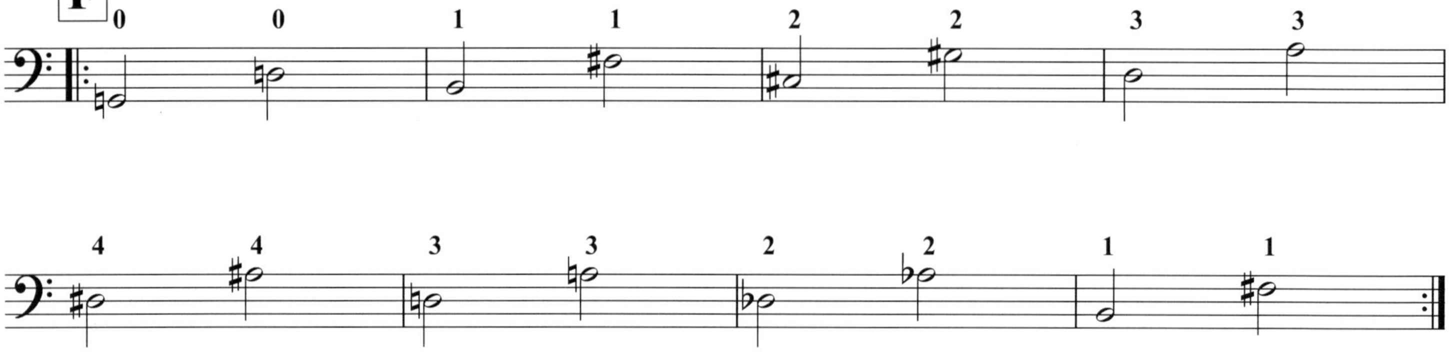

G

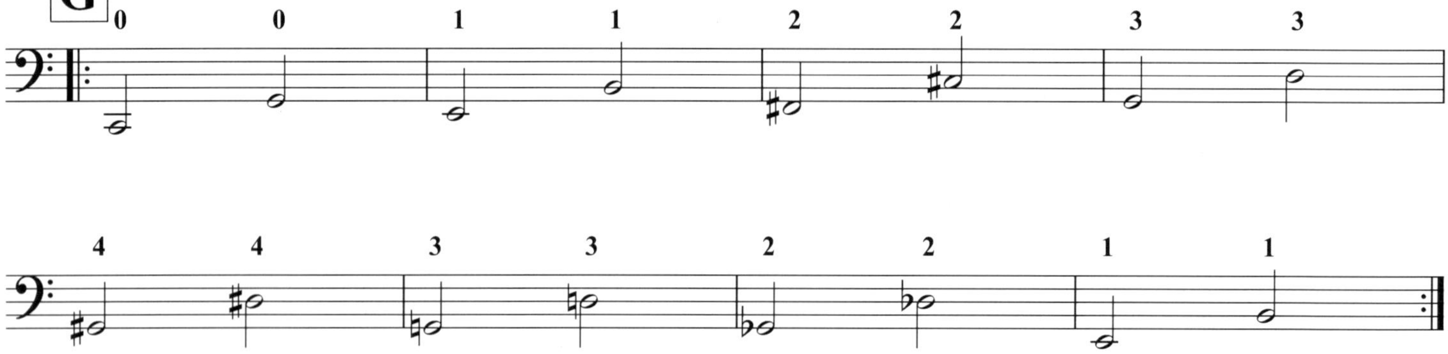

H

I

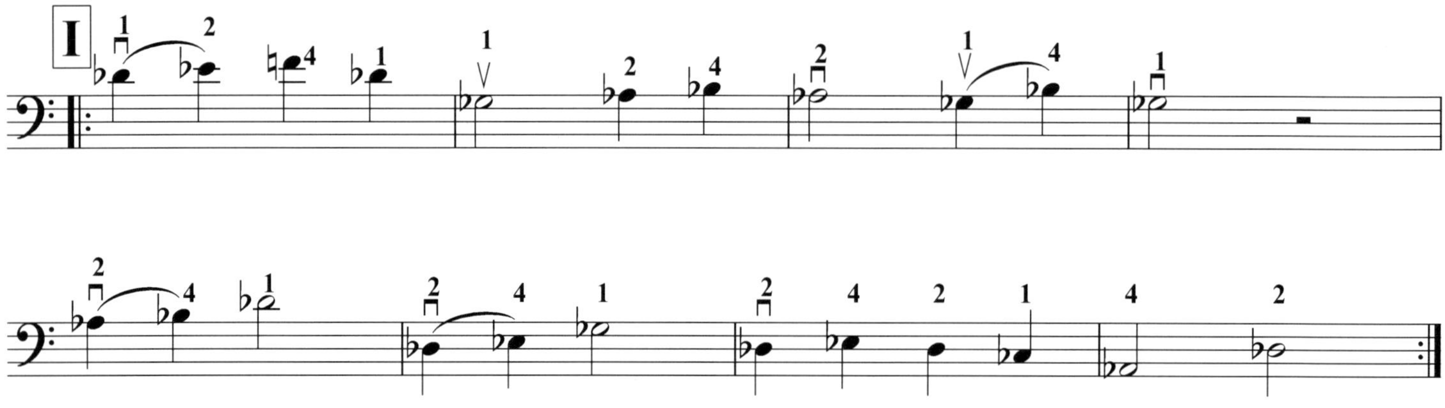

J
K
L
M
N

Lesson 7
Low Third Position

	Finger 1	Finger 2	Finger 3	Finger 4
A String	D	D♯	E	F
D String	G	G♯	A	B♭
G String	C	C♯	D	E♭
C String	F	F♯	G	A♭

In Low Third Position on the D string, your first finger goes on G, second finger on G♯ (A♭), third finger on A, and fourth finger on B♭ (A♯).

Each finger will be a half step apart.

Keep in mind: Your 1st finger is on the 4th finger tape.

Lesson 7
Exercises in Low Third Position

A

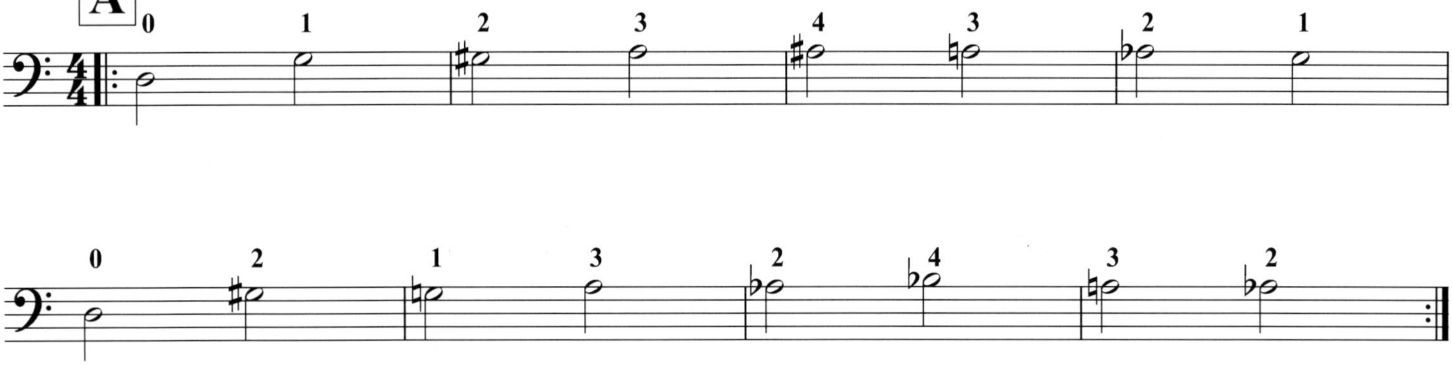

B

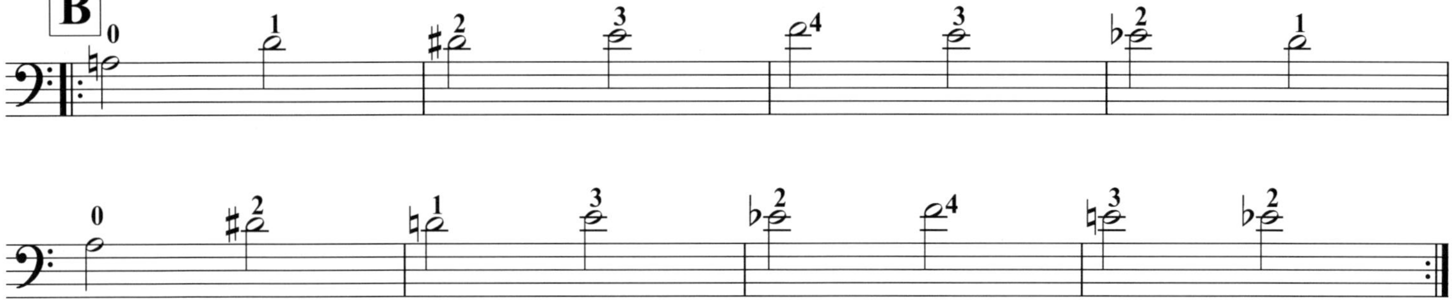

C

D

E

F

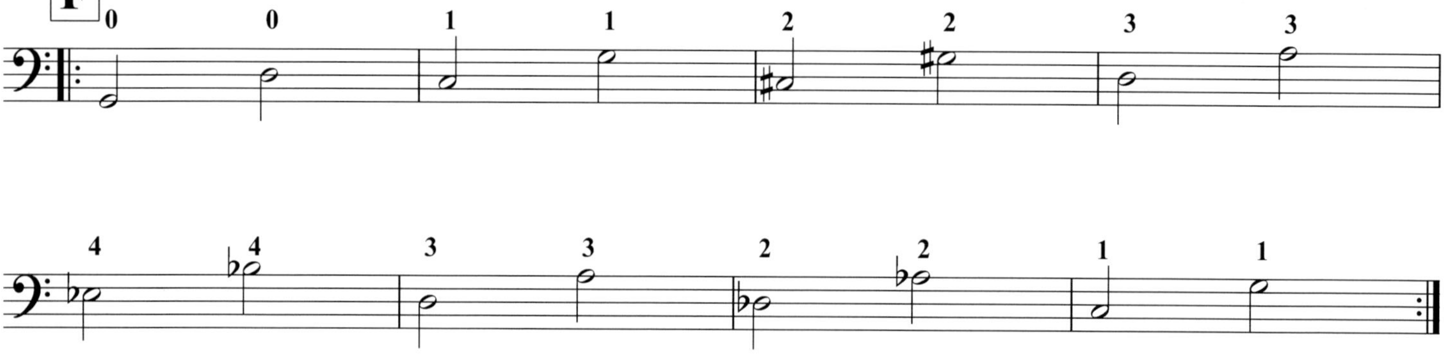

G

H

I

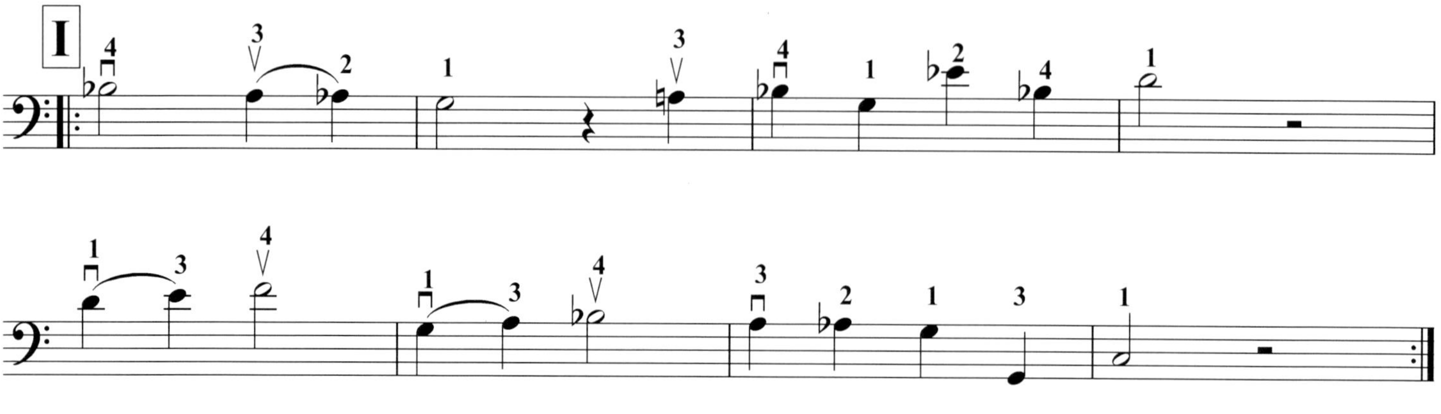

J

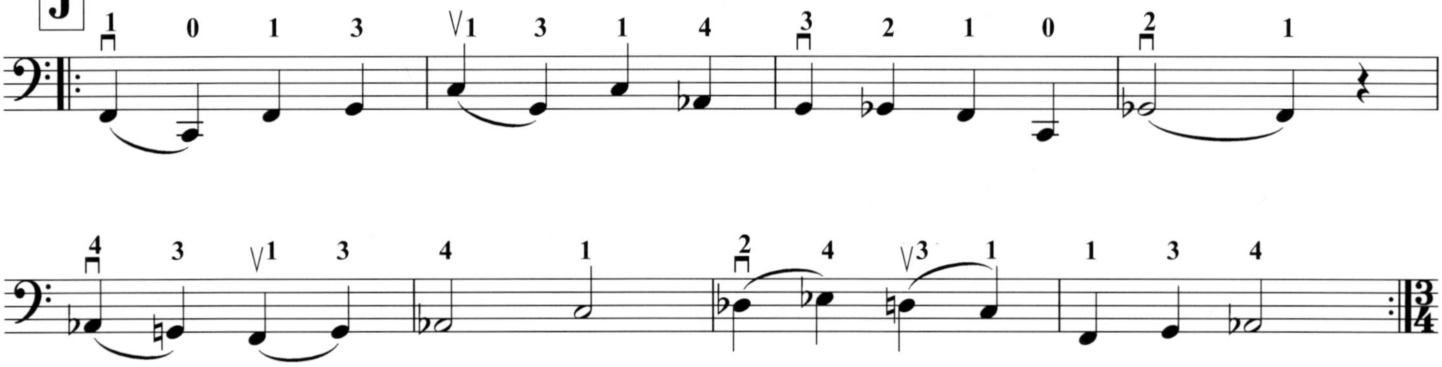

K from *Easy Classics for Cello* - "Sleeping Beauty Waltz"

L from *Corelli Cello Sonata - Opus 5, No. 8, Mvt. 1*

M from *Corelli Cello Sonata - Opus 5, No. 8, Mvt. 2*

N from *Tarantella*

O from *J. S. Bach Cello Suite No. 1, Menuetto II*

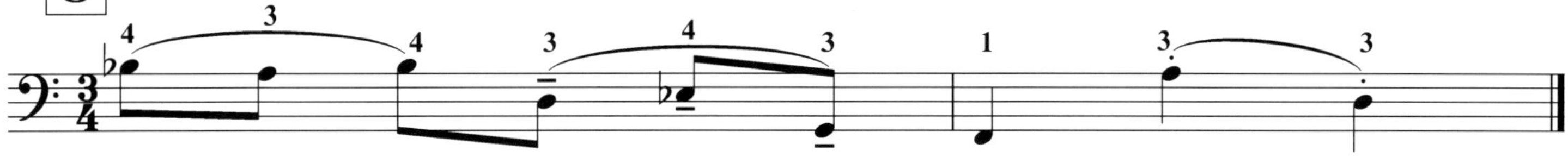

P from *J. S. Bach Cello Suite No. 3, Praeludium*

Q from *Brahms Cello Sonata - Opus 38, No. 1, Mvt. 1*

Lesson 8
Low Third Extended Position

	Finger 1	Finger 2	Finger 3	Finger 4
A String	D	E	F	F♯
D String	G	A	B♭	B
G String	C	D	E♭	E
C String	F	G	A♭	A

In Low Third Extended Position on the D string, your first finger goes on G, second finger stretches a whole step to A, third finger on B♭ (A♯), and fourth finger on B.

Each finger will be a half step apart, with the exception of the first and second finger, which will stretch a whole step.

Keep in mind: Your 1st finger is still on the 4th finger tape.

Lesson 8
Exercises in Low Third Extended Position

A

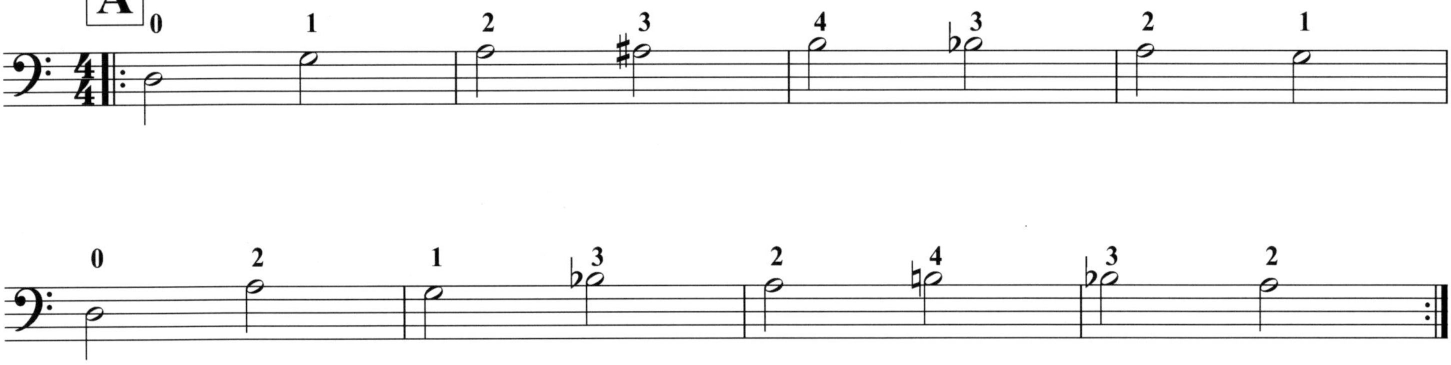

B

C

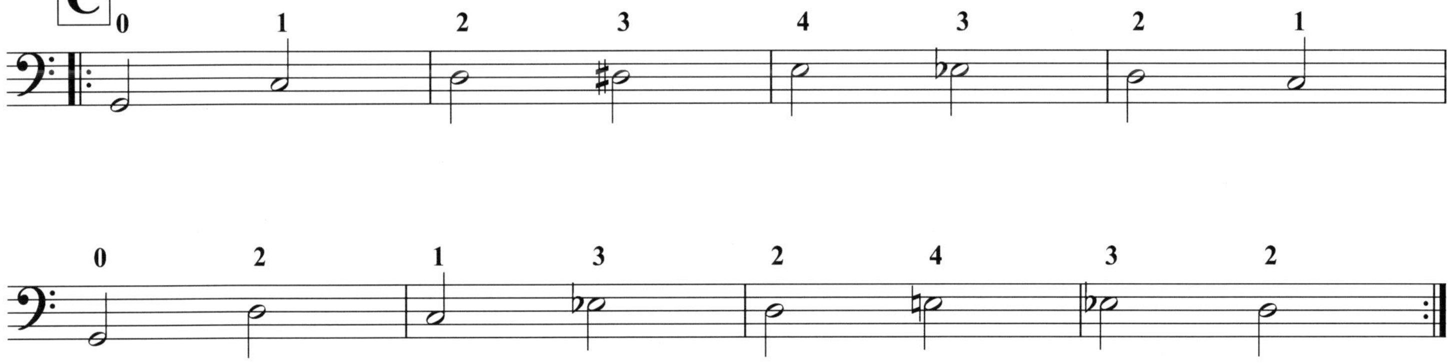

D

E

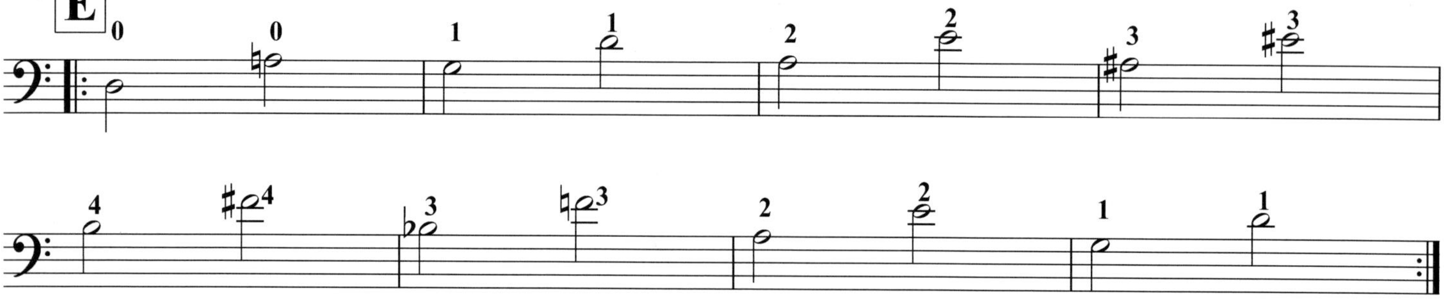

F

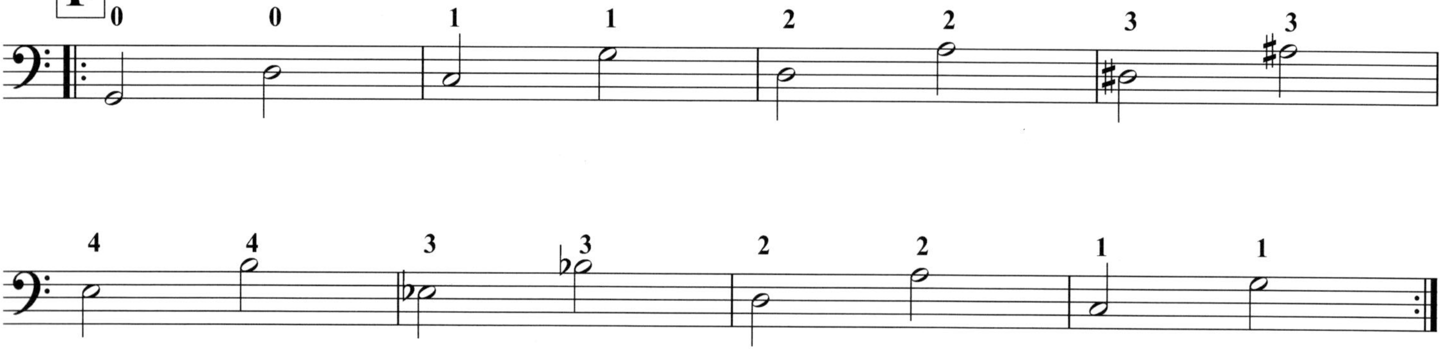

G

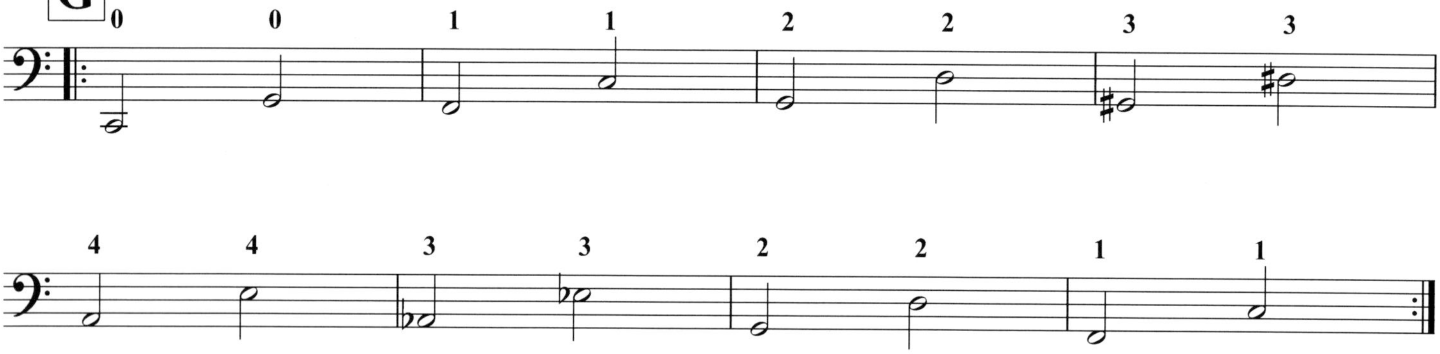

H

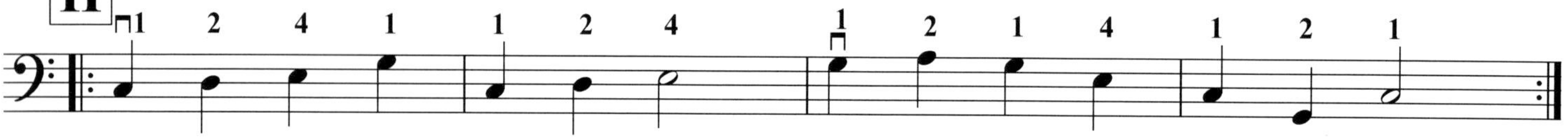

I

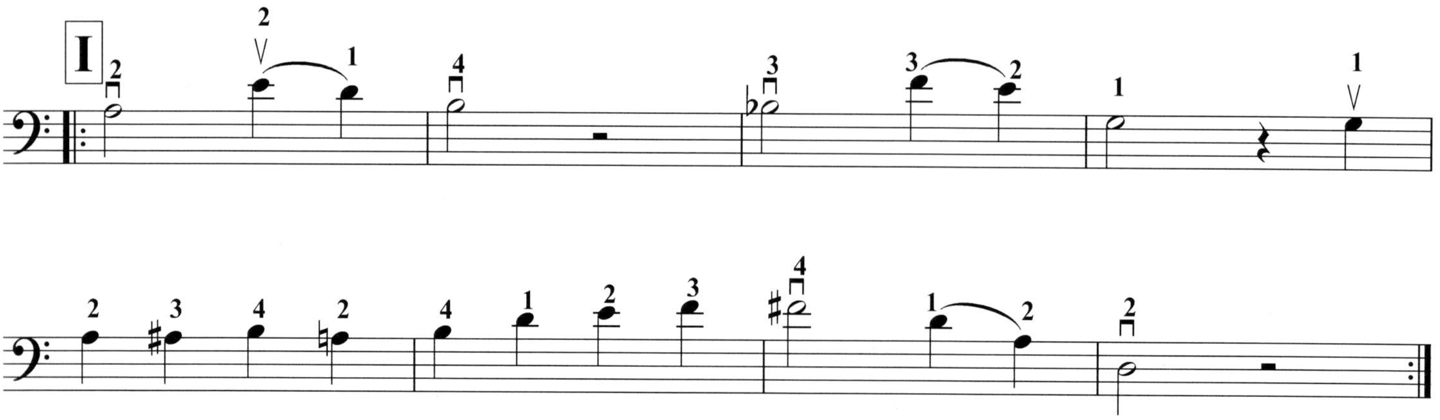

J

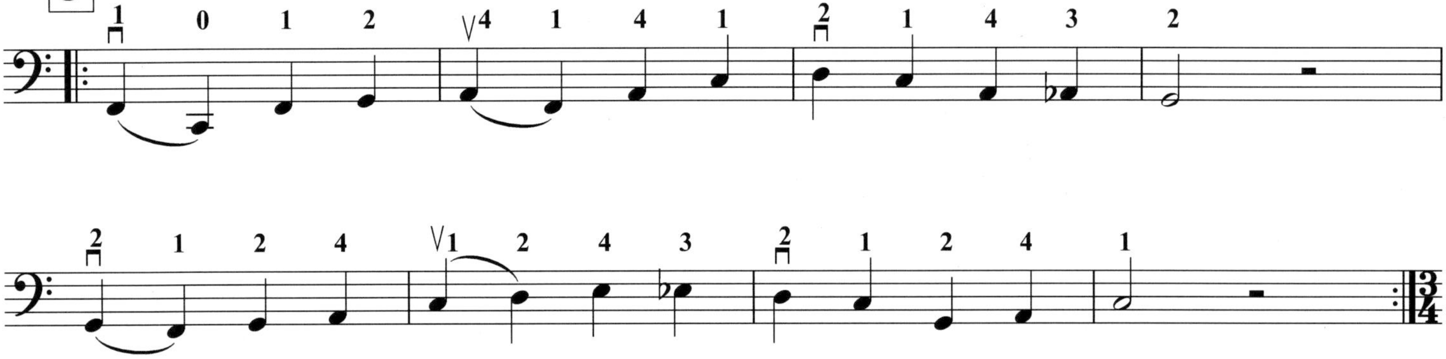

K

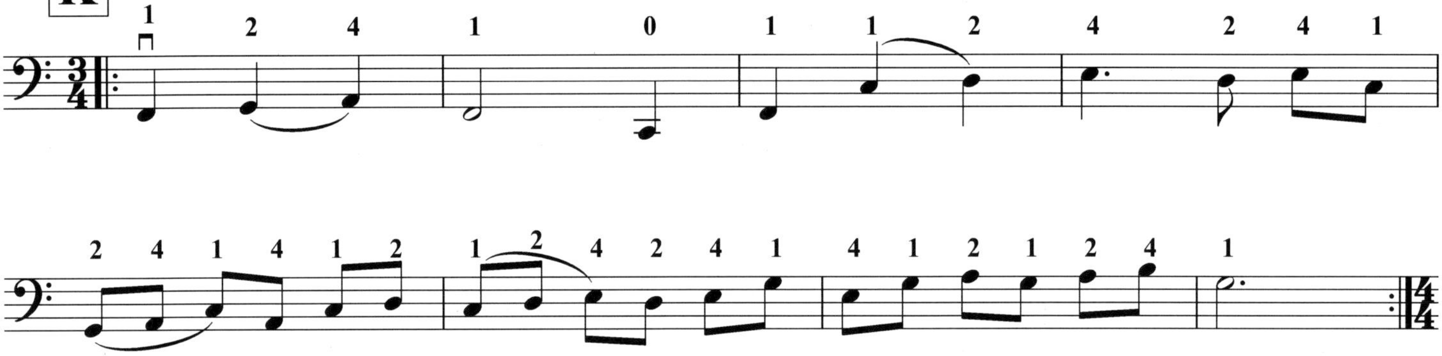

L from *The Fiddling Cellist* - "Bill Cheatham"

M from *The Fiddling Cellist* - "Sheebeg, Sheemore" duet

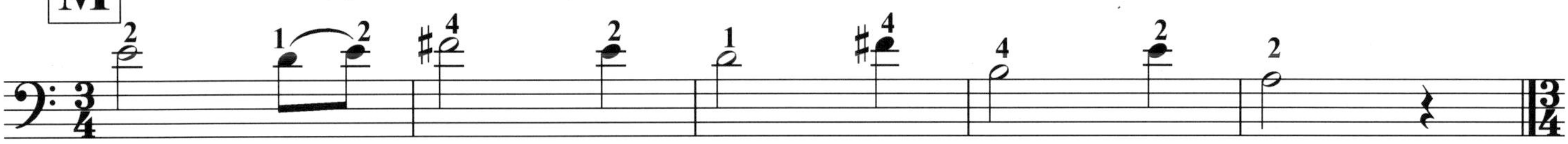

N from *The Fiddling Cellist* - "Down in the Willow Garden" variation

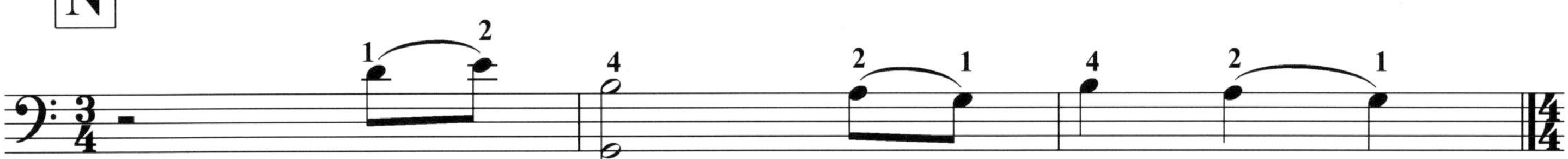

O from *101 Easy Songs for Cello* - "Largo" by Dvořák

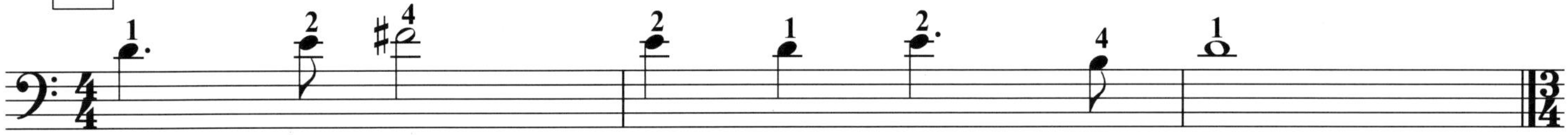

P from *J. S. Bach Cello Suite 1, Mvt. 3*

Lesson 9
High Third Position

	Finger 1	Finger 2	Finger 3	Finger 4
A String	E♭	E	F	F♯
D String	A♭	A	B♭	B
G String	D♭	D	E♭	E
C String	G♭	G	A♭	A

In High Third Position on the D string, your first finger goes on G♯ (A♭), second finger on A, third finger on B♭ (A♯), and fourth finger on B.

Each finger will be a half step apart.

Keep in mind: The only finger on a tape is your 2nd finger!

Lesson 9
Exercises in High Third Position

A

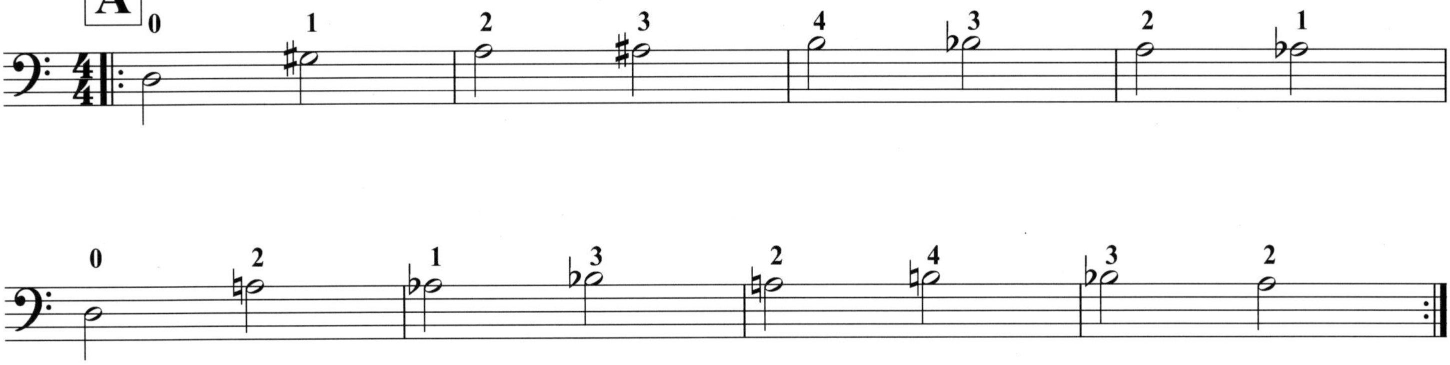

B

C

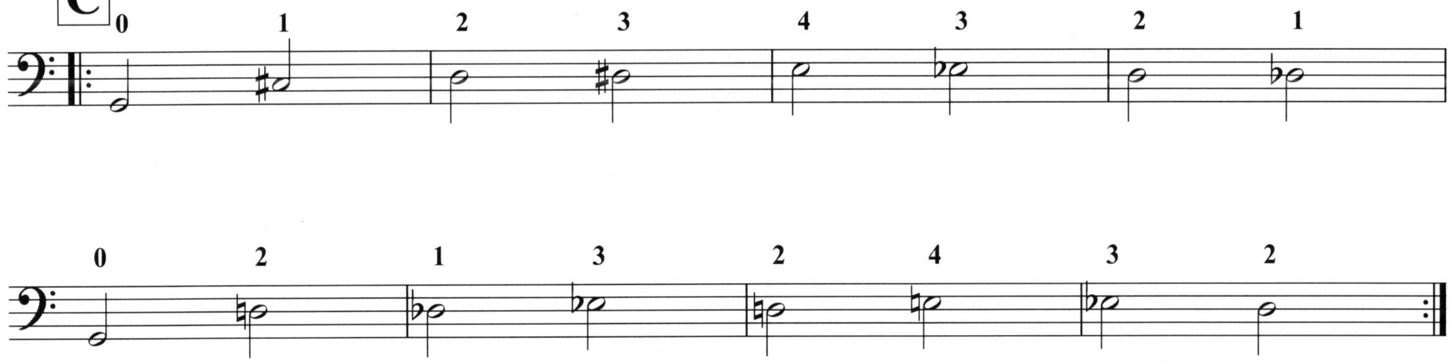

D

E
F
G
H
I

J

K

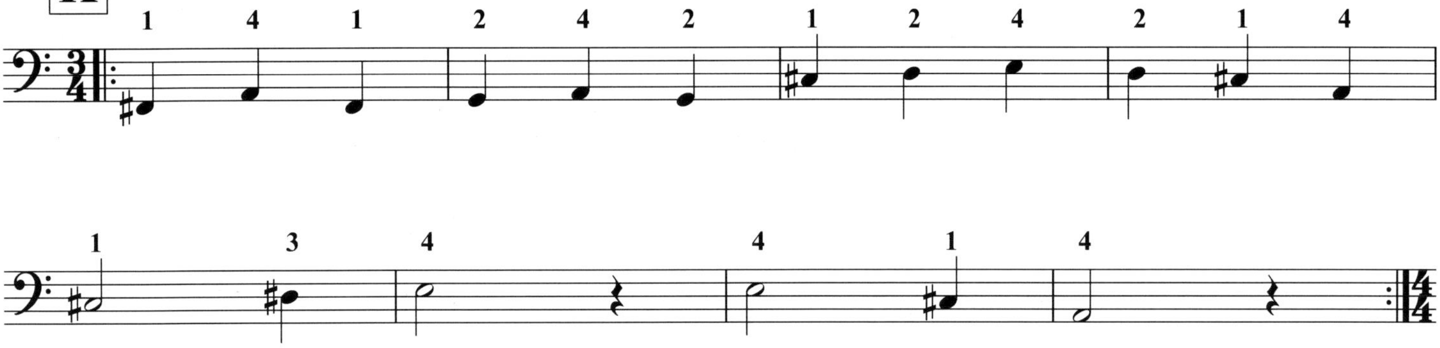

L

M from *Easy Classics for Cello* - "Hungarian Dance #5"

N from *Breval Cello Sonata - Opus 40, No. 1, Mvt. 1*

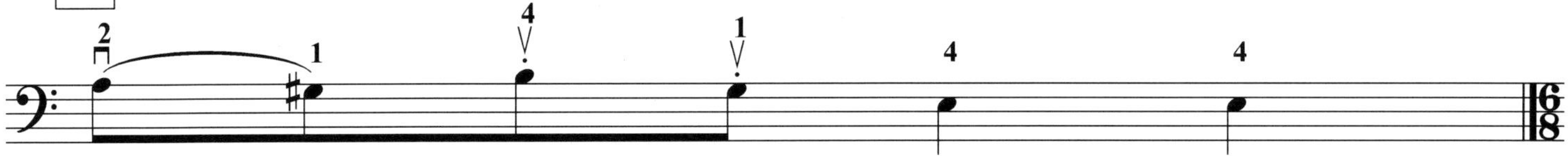

O from *Tarantella*

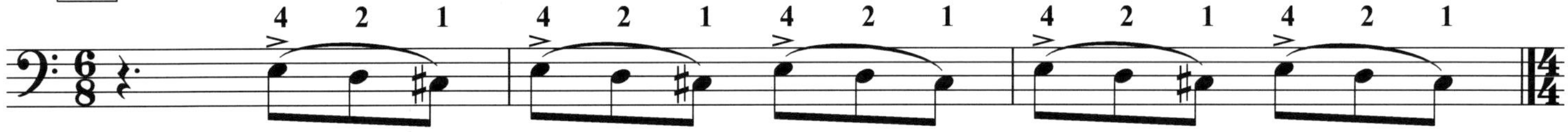

P from *Brahms Cello Sonata - Opus 38, No. 1, Mvt. 3*

Lesson 10
High Third Extended Position

	Finger 1	Finger 2	Finger 3	Finger 4
A String	E♭	F	F♯	G
D String	A♭	B♭	B	C
G String	D♭	E♭	E	F
C String	G♭	A♭	A	B♭

In High Third Extended Position on the D string, your first finger goes on G♯ (A♭), second finger stretches a whole step to A♯ (B♭), third finger on B, and fourth finger on C.

Each finger will be a half step apart, with the exception of the first and second finger, which will stretch a whole step.

Keep in mind: In this position, we skip right over the open string replacer notes. Also, your thumb can go in the "cello neck nook" as described in the next lesson.

Lesson 10
Exercises in High Third Extended Position

A

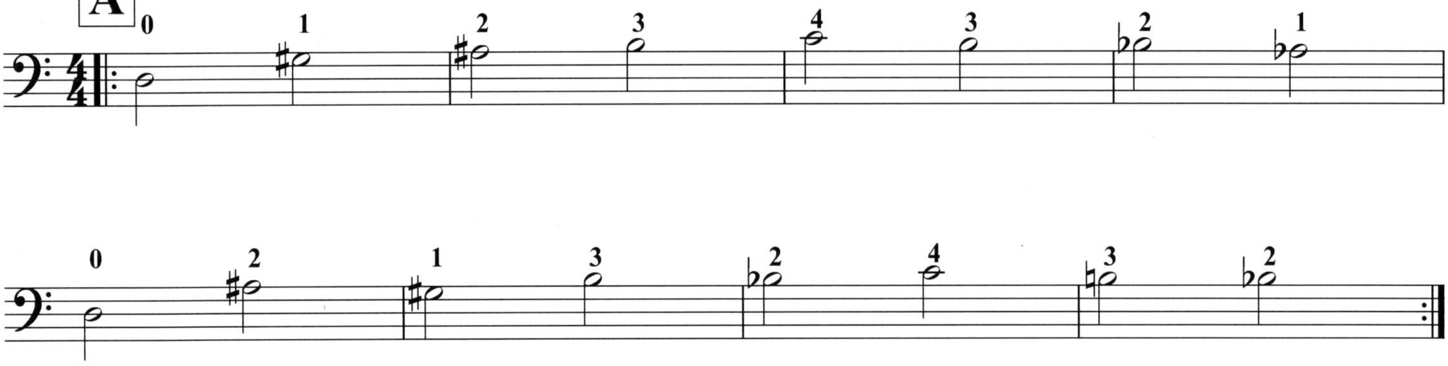

B

C

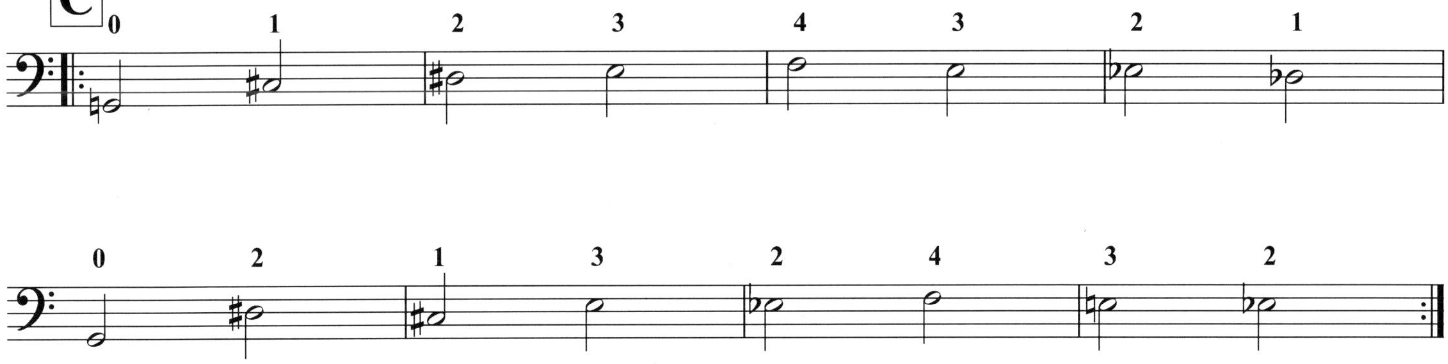

D

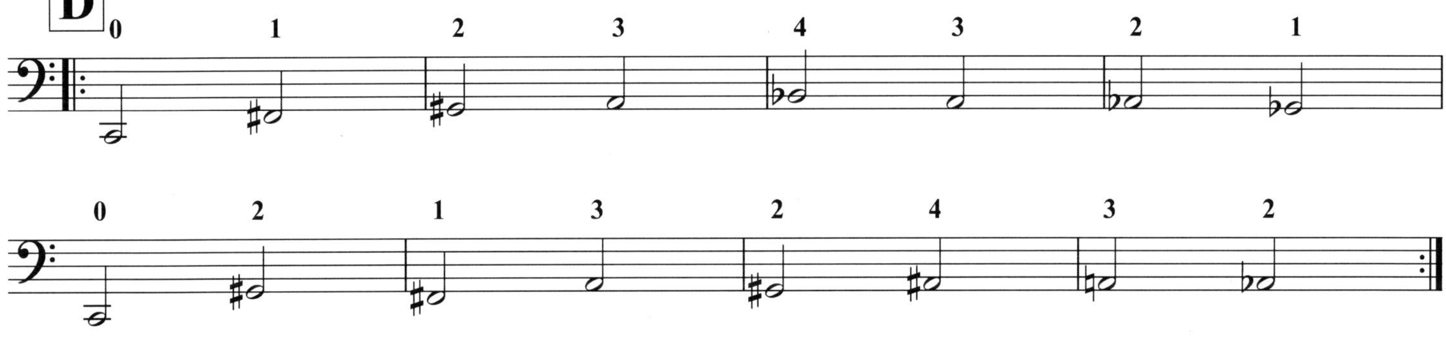

E
F
G
H
I

J

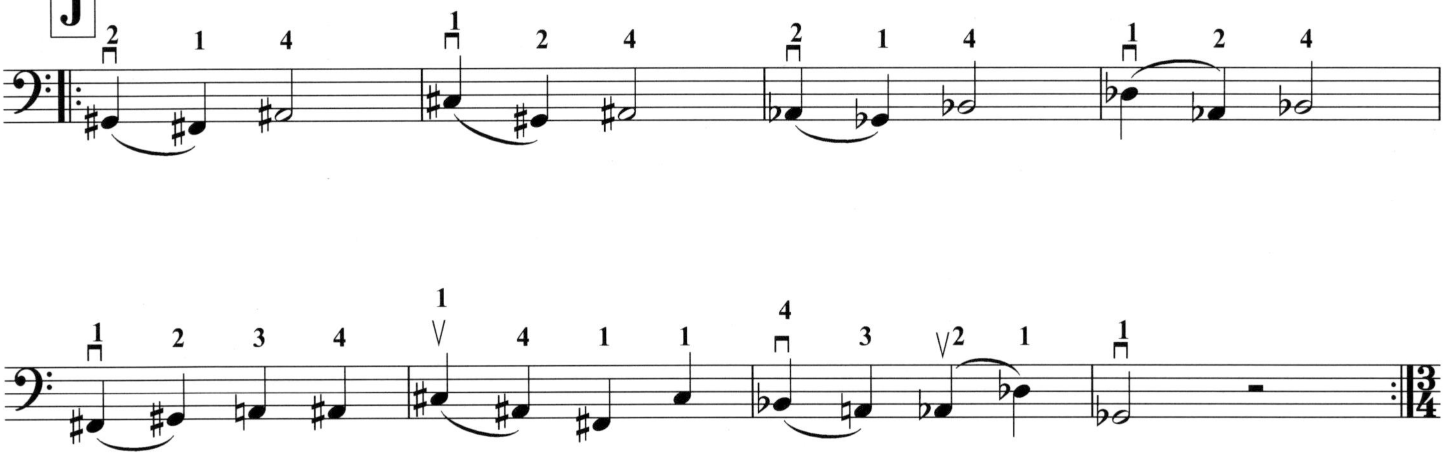

K

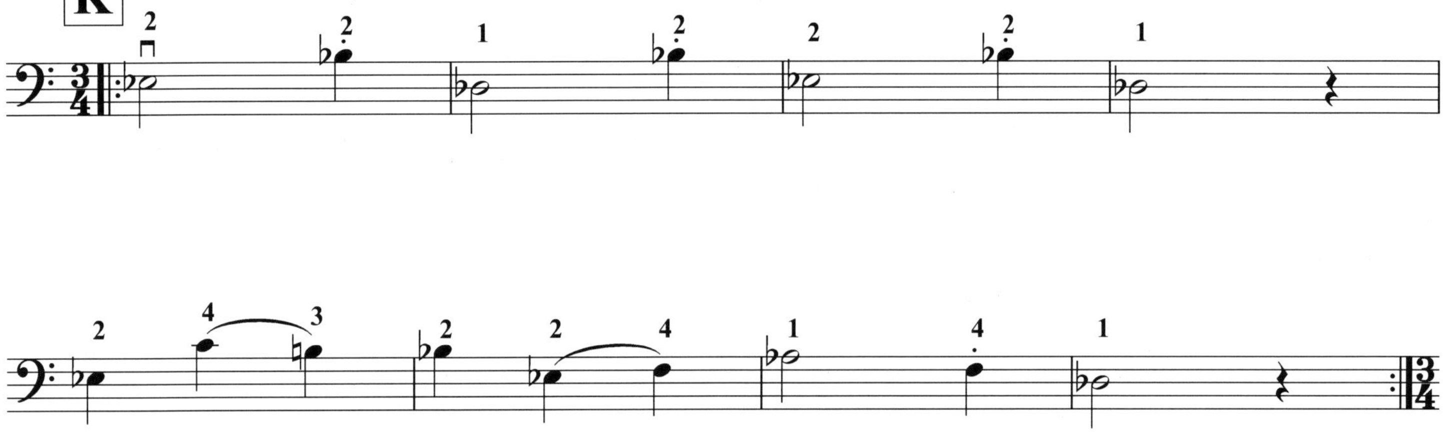

L

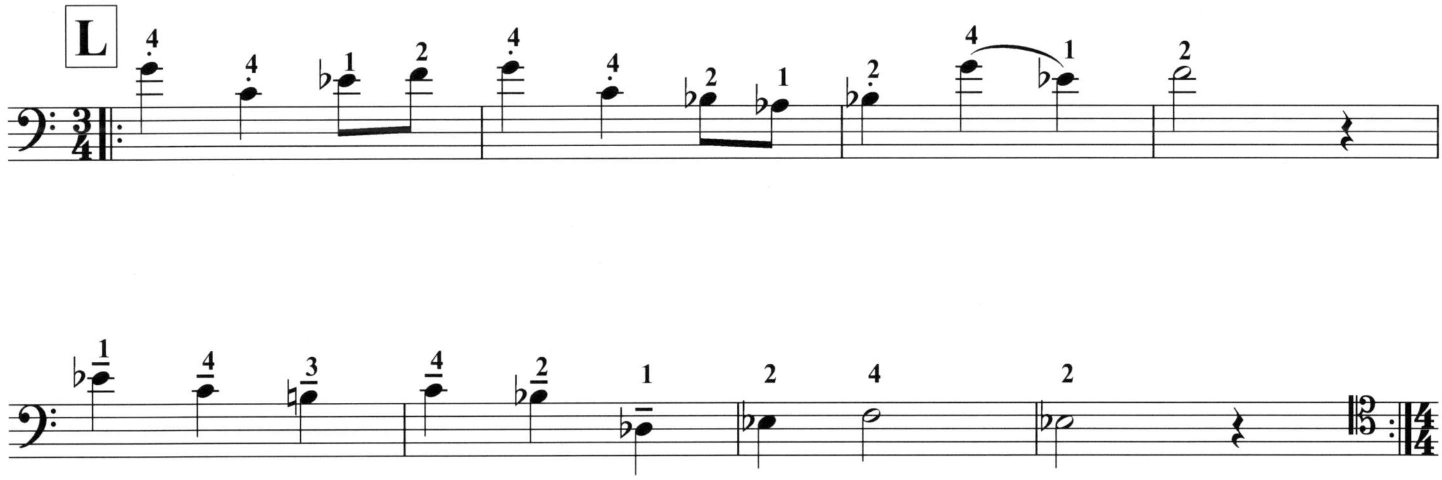

M from *Brahms Cello Sonata - Opus 38, No. 1, Mvt. 1*

Lesson 11
Fourth Position

	Finger 1	Finger 2	Finger 3	Finger 4
A String	E	F	F♯	G
D String	A	B♭	B	C
G String	D	E♭	E	F
C String	G	A♭	A	B♭

In Fourth Position on the D string, your first finger goes on A, second finger on B♭ (A♯), third finger on B, and fourth finger on C.

This is a special position because we are given an advantage: in this position, your thumb can go right in the "nook" of the cello neck. Every cello is different, and everyone's hands are different, so take some time to learn where your cello's neck nook is in relation to your first finger note and what that feels like.

Each finger will be a half step apart.

Keep in mind: Your 1st finger, in "the nook", is now replacing open strings.

Lesson 11
Exercises in Fourth Position

A

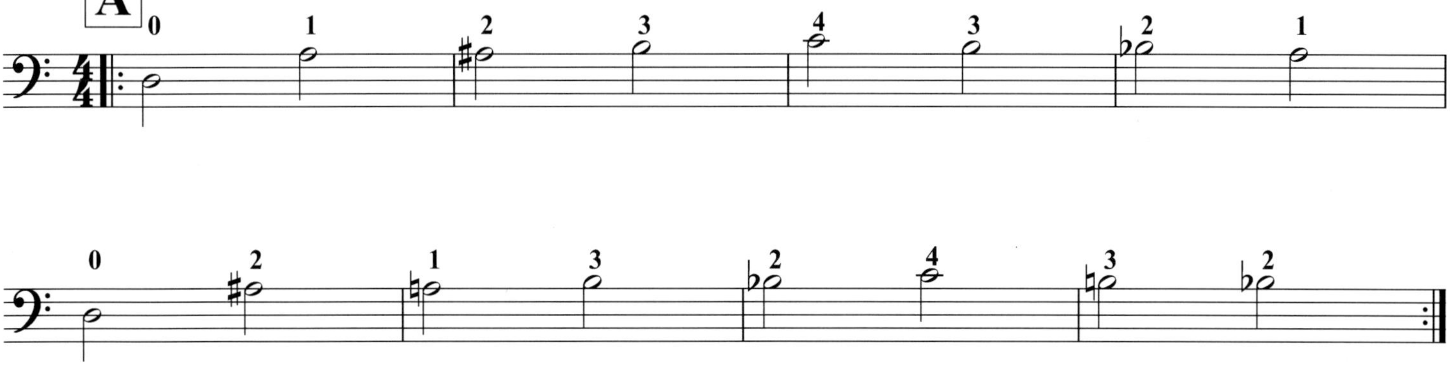

B

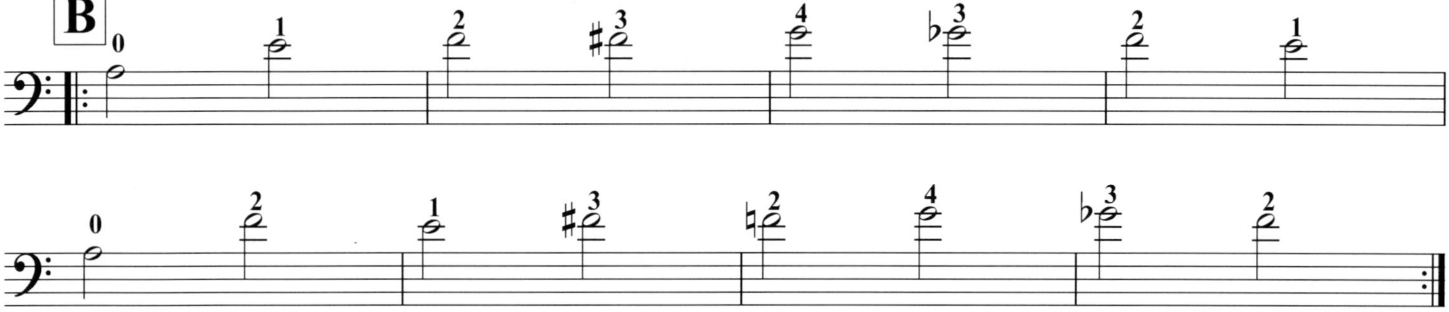

C

D

E
F
G
H
I

J

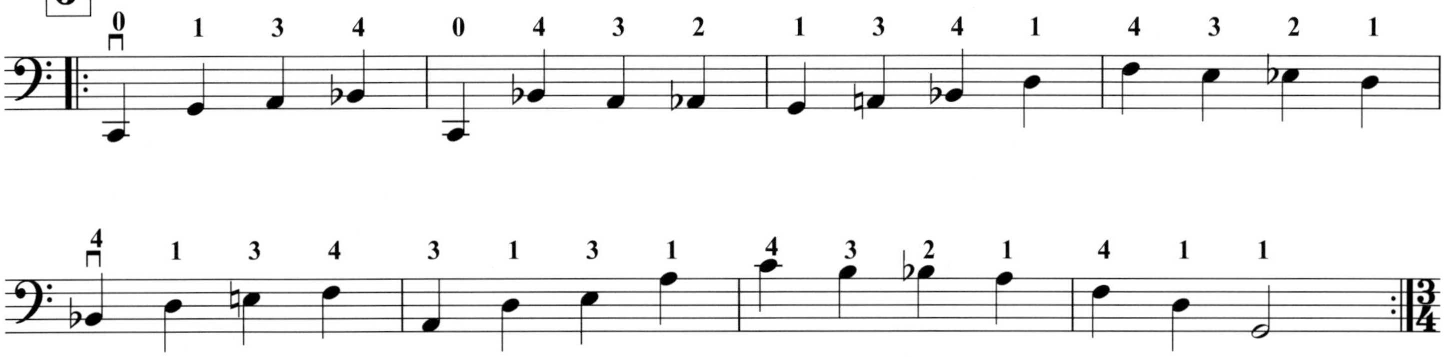

K from *The Fiddling Cellist* - "Sheebeg, Sheemore"

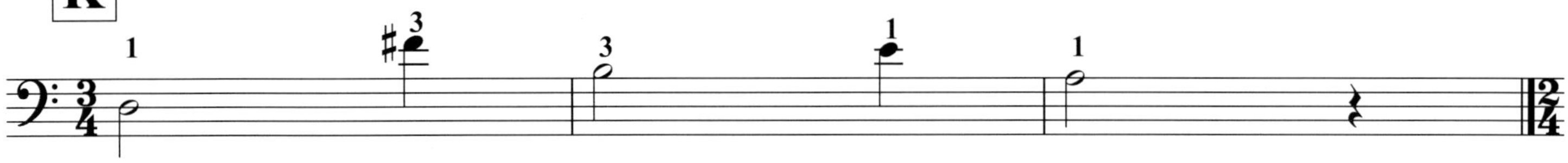

L from *Breval Cello Sonata - Opus 40, No. 2, Mvt. 2*

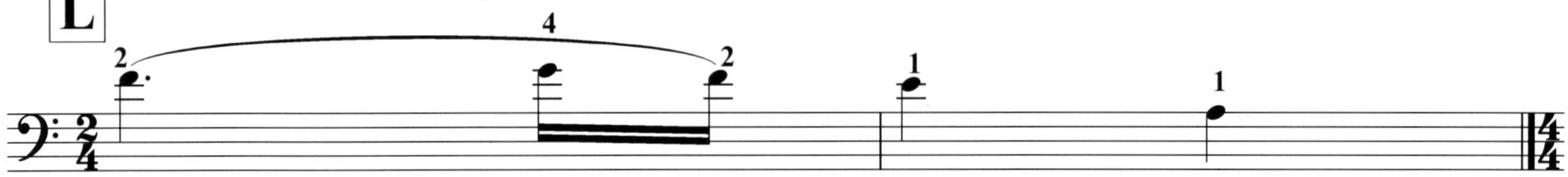

M from *Corelli Cello Sonata - Opus 5, No. 8, Mvt. 2*

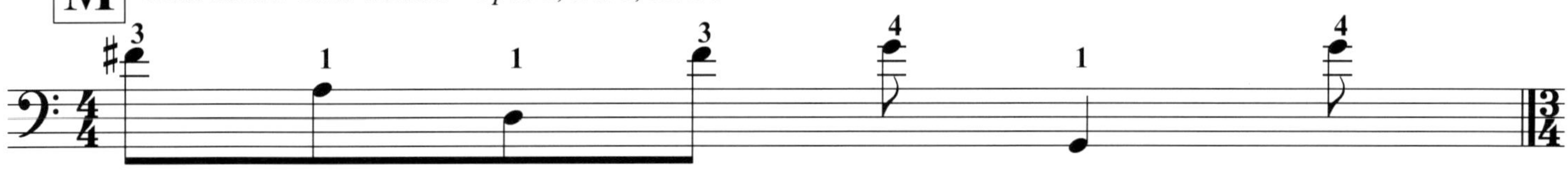

N from *Eccles Cello Sonata in G Minor*

O from *Tarantella*

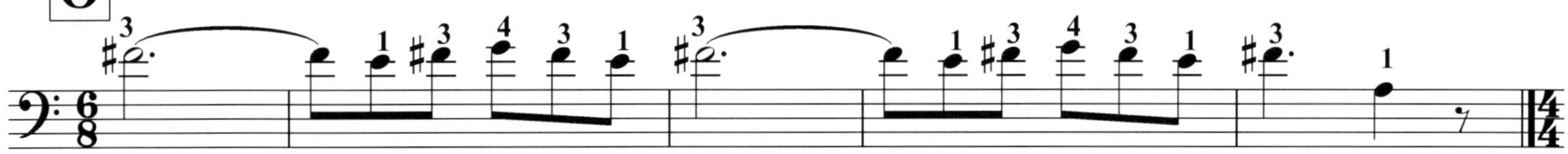

P from *J. S. Bach Cello Suite No. 1, Mvt. 1*

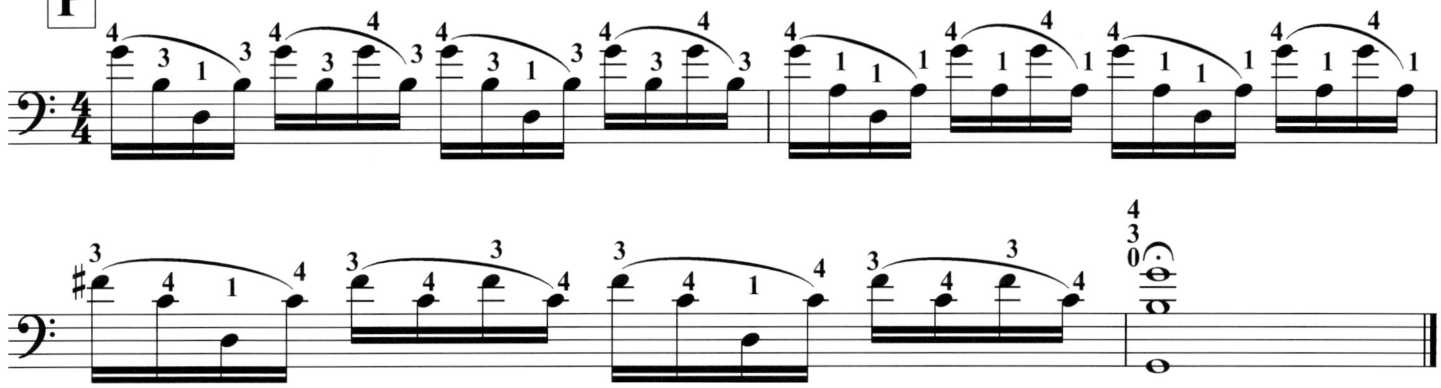

Lesson 12
Fourth Extended Position

	Finger 1	Finger 2	Finger 3	Finger 4
A String	E	F♯	G	G♯
D String	A	B	C	C♯
G String	D	E	F	F♯
C String	G	A	B♭	B

In Fourth Extended Position on the D string, your first finger goes on A, second finger on B,third finger on C, and fourth finger on C♯ (D♭).

Your thumb can stay in the "nook" here!

Lesson 12
Exercises in Fourth Extended Position

A

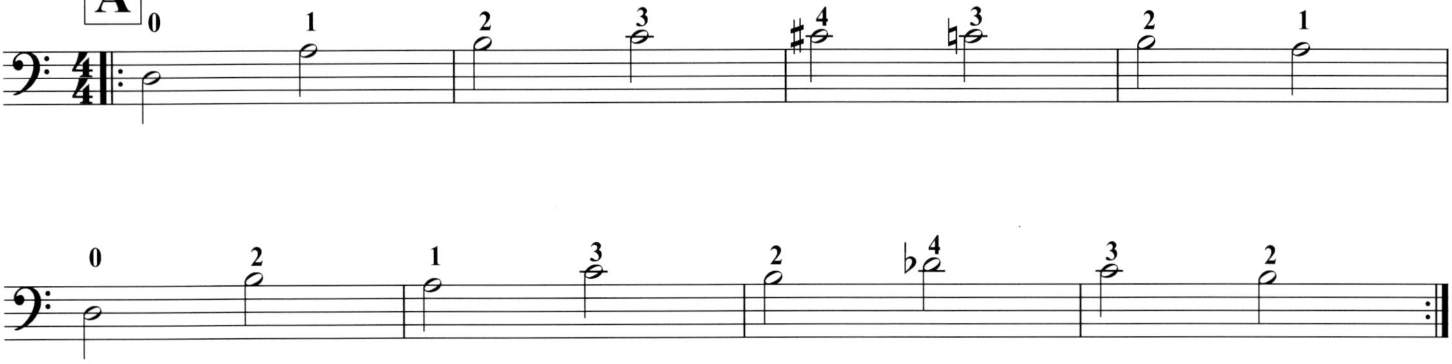

B

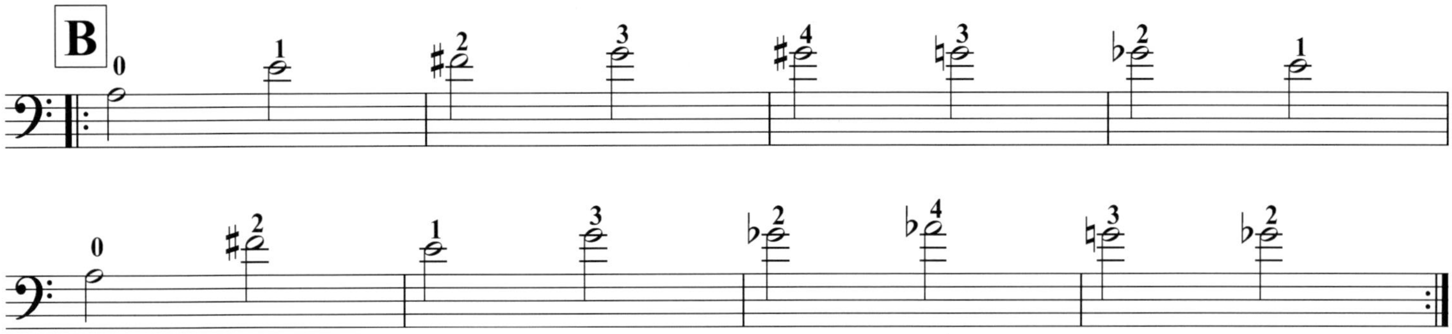

C

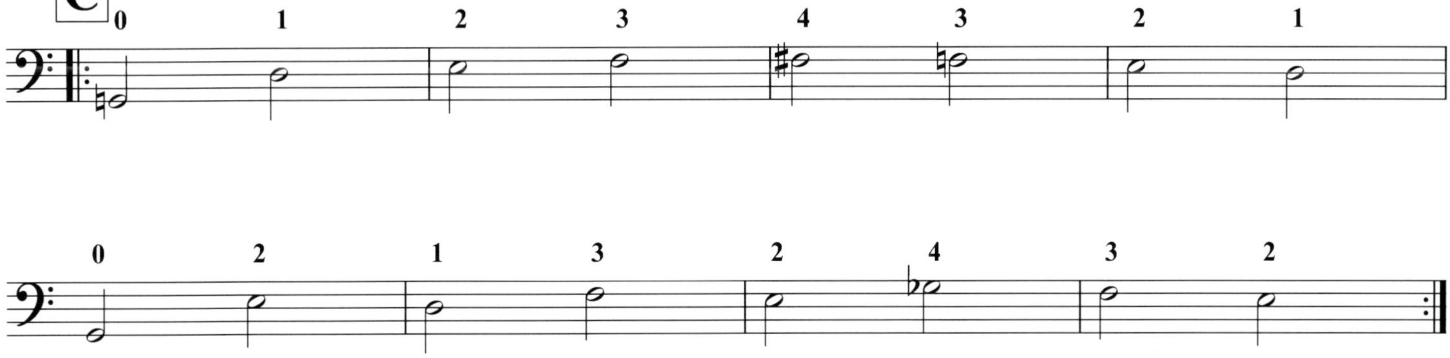

D

E

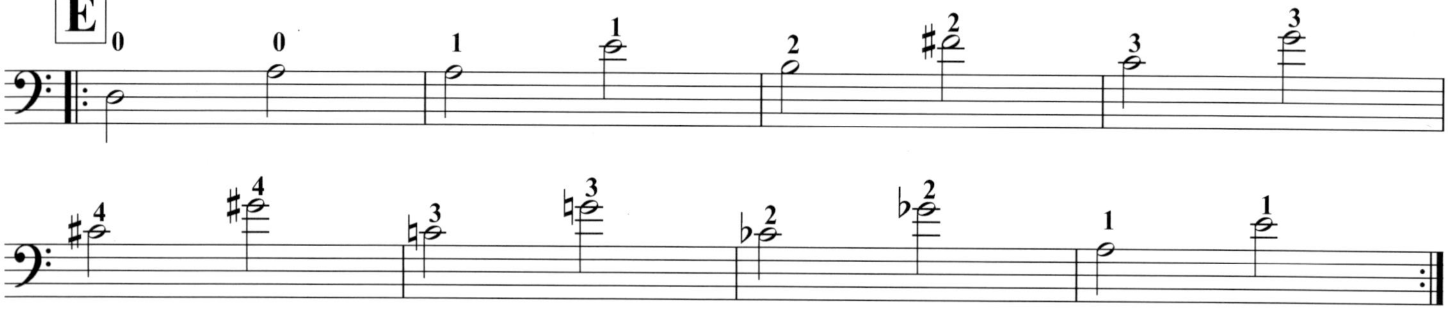

F

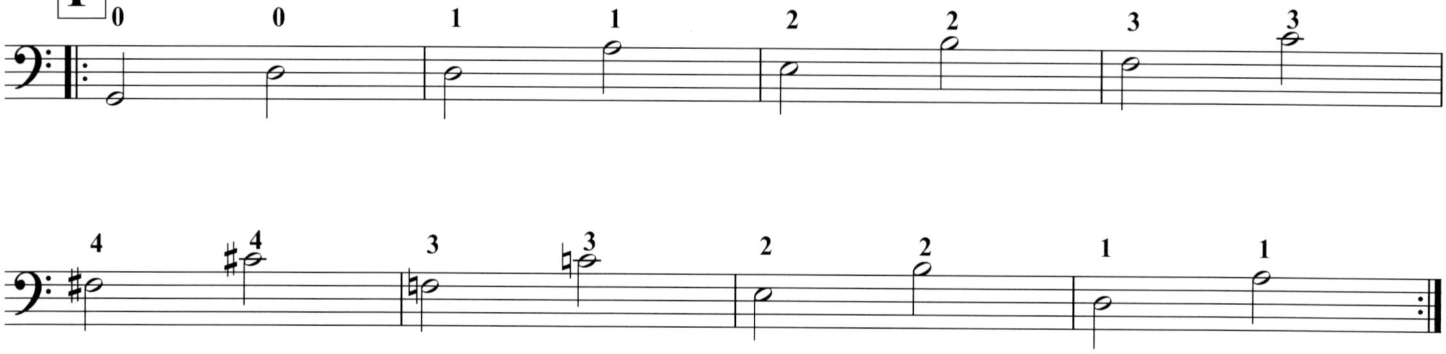

G

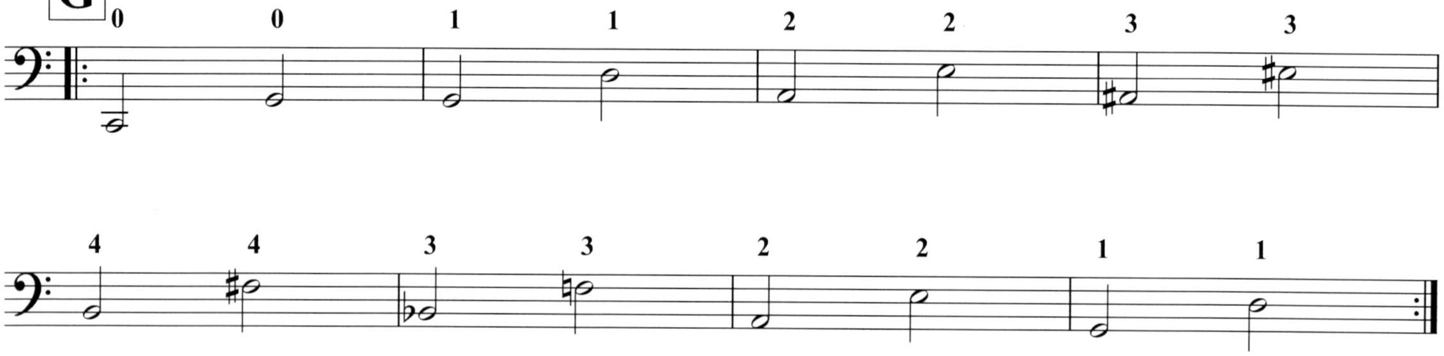

H

I

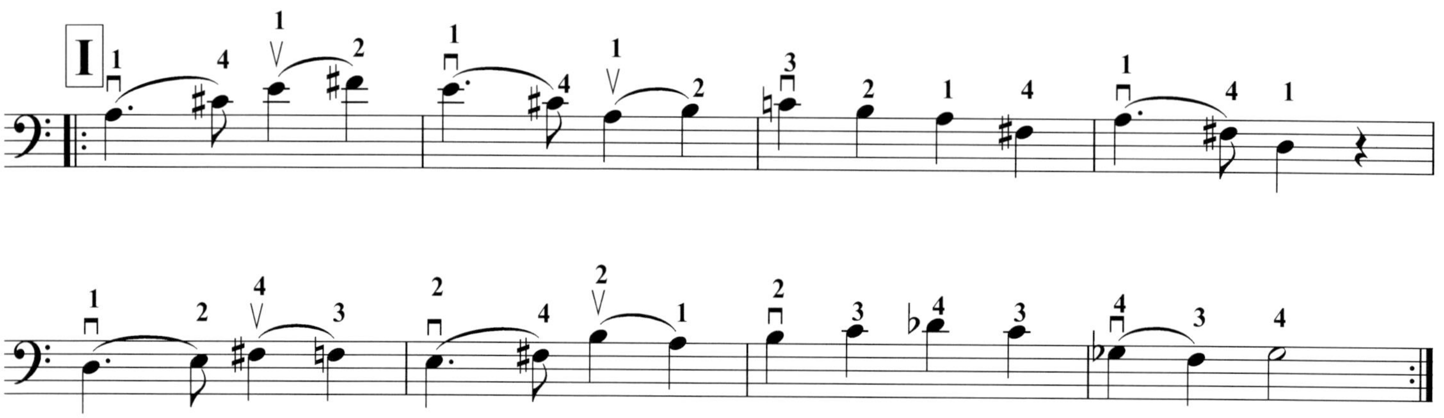

J

K

L

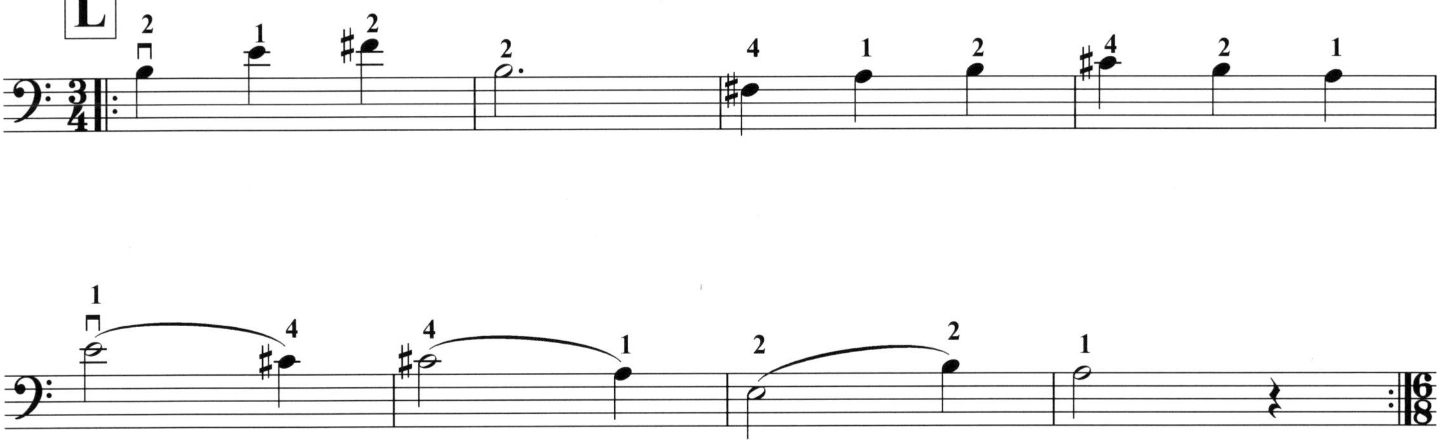

M from *Tarantella*

Halley Feaster

Halley Feaster is a contemporary and Classical acoustic and electric cellist, with a dual Bachelor's degree from Berklee College of Music in Performance and Professional Music (2009). While in Boston, she enjoyed recording session work and was chosen to perform with Gloria Estefan, Steve Winwood, Philip Bailey, the Jon Finn Group, and Herbie Hancock. She was also the string arranger and coordinator for the American Celtic punk band, the Dropkick Murphys, with credits on several albums as well as live performances with DKM on their St. Patrick's Day Boston shows and northeast tours.

Halley greatly values the power of music education and is very thankful to have studied with teachers who opened worlds of art and opportunities in her youth. She hopes to pass along her passion and knowledge by teaching students of all levels and ages.

Congratulations!

You have mastered Half to Fourth positions!

You are now ready to move on to Volume 2 of the Cello Position Handbook!

Also, check out some of these pieces that you can practice your new position knowledge with:

-Breval Cello Sonata in C Major, Opus 40, No. 1
-Squire Danse Rustique, Opus 20, No. 5
-Klengel Sonatina No. 1 in C minor, Opus 48

Thank you for practicing with me,
and best wishes on your cello technique journey!

Other Mel Bay Cello Books

Other Mel Bay Cello Books

My Very Best Christmas: Cello (Khanagov)
New Acoustic Music for Folk Engemble (The Moonrakers)
Sacred Melodies for Solo Cello (C. Duncan)
Scottish Melodies for Two Cellos (Witt)
Student's Book of Rounds: Cello (Worth)
The Fiddling Cellist (Bratt)
The Student Cellist: Bach (C. Duncan)
The Student Cellist: Beethoven (C. Duncan)
The Student Cellist: Handel (C. Duncan)
The Student Cellist: Mozart (C. Duncan)
Wedding Music for Solo Cello (Curatolo)
Winter-Violin & Cello (Parks & Groschan Jazz Cello Wizard, Jr. Book 2 (Norgaard)
Music from Around the World for Solo & Ensemble: Cello/Bass (Miller)
My Very Best Christmas: Cello (Khanagov)
New Acoustic Music for Folk Engemble (The Moonrakers)
Sacred Melodies for Solo Cello (C. Duncan)
Scottish Melodies for Two Cellos (Witt)
Student's Book of Rounds: Cello (Worth)
The Fiddling Cellist (Bratt)
The Student Cellist: Bach (C. Duncan)
The Student Cellist: Beethoven (C. Duncan)
The Student Cellist: Handel (C. Duncan)
The Student Cellist: Mozart (C. Duncan)
Wedding Music for Solo Cello (Curatolo)
Winter-Violin & Cello (Parks & Groschang)
Beginner Cello Theory for Children Book 1 (M. Smith)
Beginner Cello Theory for Children Book 2 (M. Smith)
Beginner Cello Theory for Children Book 3 (M. Smith)
Cello Chords, Rhythms and Backups for Fiddle Tunes (Bratt)
Cello Wall Chart (Norgaard)
Practice for Performance (Morganstern)
Progressive Scale Studies for Cello (Bauer)
Technical Studies for Beginning Cello Level 1 (C. Duncan)
The Art of Scales (Cunningham)
The Fiddling Cellist (Bratt)

WWW.MELBAY.COM